丽江师范高等专科学校资助出版

EANLIC English Public Speaking Training Course

英力克英语演讲教程

主　编　杨慧梅　段平华　唐　湖
副主编　朱　俊　张庆梅　谷　兰
参　编　和　婷　周丽云　邓丽萍

苏州大学出版社

图书在版编目(CIP)数据

英力克英语演讲教程 = EANLIC English Public Speaking Training Course / 杨慧梅,段平华,唐湖主编. —苏州:苏州大学出版社,2024.4
ISBN 978-7-5672-4759-8

Ⅰ.①英… Ⅱ.①杨… ②段… ③唐… Ⅲ.①英语-演讲-教材 Ⅳ.①H311.9

中国国家版本馆 CIP 数据核字(2024)第 062400 号

书　　名:	英力克英语演讲教程
	YINGLIKE YINGYU YANJIANG JIAOCHENG
主　　编:	杨慧梅　段平华　唐　湖
责任编辑:	沈　琴
装帧设计:	刘　俊　司马林青
出版发行:	苏州大学出版社(Soochow University Press)
社　　址:	苏州市十梓街1号　邮编:215006
印　　刷:	江苏图美云印刷科技有限公司
邮购热线:	0512-67480030
销售热线:	0512-67481020
开　　本:	787 mm×1 092 mm　1/16　印张:13.25　字数:268千
版　　次:	2024年4月第1版
印　　次:	2024年4月第1次印刷
书　　号:	ISBN 978-7-5672-4759-8
定　　价:	68.00元

图书若有印装错误,本社负责调换
苏州大学出版社营销部　电话:0512-67481020
苏州大学出版社网址　http://www.sudapress.com
苏州大学出版社邮箱　sdcbs@suda.edu.cn

　　《英力克英语演讲教程》是为大学英语学习者所编写的一本实用性和人文性兼备的教材。本教材的编写依据教育部《教育部关于全面提高高等教育质量的若干意见》《高等学校课程思政建设指导纲要》《中国教育现代化2035》等相关规定，充分考虑现代外语教学理论和实践，采用成果导向教育（OBE）和以学生为中心的任务型教学方法，通过改革教学目标、教学内容、教学方法等方面，提高教学质量和教学效果，以期全面提升学生英语口语表达能力。

　　自2004年，丽江师范高等专科学校就开始对英语教学进行了改革，率先提出并试行了英力克（EANLIC）英语习得模式，并在传统英语口语课程的基础上，创设了英力克英语口语课程。"EANLIC"是"English Acquired as a Native Language in China"的缩略语，其本质是为英语学习者创造一个英语语言环境，让他们沉浸其中，自然而然地习得英语。本教材正是通过英力克英语口语课程的整个教学过程，系统地为学生创建一个良好的英语语言输入和输出环境，以期更好地帮助学生提高英语语言应用能力。

　　与传统的英语口语教材相比，本教材教学内容丰富，汲取了TED演讲的精华，侧重思想教育，注重培养学生的综合素质，帮助学生树立正确的人生观、世界观和价值观。选材上重点关注学生个人成长和品格塑造，帮助学生拓宽视野，加深对世界的了解，更好地领悟人生的哲理，同时快速提高英语口语表达能力。

　　与传统的英语口语教材相比，本教材从演讲前的准备工作、演讲中的语言技巧，到演讲后的总结和反思，每一个环节都有详细的指导和实用的技巧，并对教学目标、教学内容和教学方法进行了改革。其中，教学目标还包括了课程思政方面的目标，旨在引导学生树立正确的人生观、世界观和价值观，培养爱国主义意识，充分体现思想教育的功能。因英语演讲的即时性和临场性，口语表达中会出现少量不符合常规表达的现象，为尊重演讲者，尽量完整、真实地呈现了演讲的原文。

在本教材的编写过程中，我们力求创新，注重实用，充分吸取了各方专家和学生的意见和建议，旨在为在校大学生，为广大英语学习者，也为希望在职场或在学术界更自如地用英语演讲和在社交场合中更好地用英语展示自己的朋友，提供一本实用、高效、科学的英语演讲培训教材。希望有更多的英语学习者能够通过本教材的学习，找到适合自己的学习方法，提高自身的英语口语表达能力，从而为个人的发展创造更多的机会，也为我们国家和世界的发展做出更大的贡献。

花 蓉

华东师范大学

教学指南

经过多轮试用、修改和调整，《英力克英语演讲教程》终于可以面世了！为了用好本教材，师生在开展教学之前，有必要研读并熟悉以下内容。

一、编写理念和教学模式

第一，本教材的编写理念基于英力克英语习得模式。英力克是英文EANLIC（English Acquired as a Native Language in China）的音译中文，是丽江师范高等专科学校外国语学院于2004年首创的一种英语习得模式，其理念是要在中国这样一个非英语国家的一定时间、空间和人群范围内，人为地创造出一种类似于英语母语者的语言运用环境，使学生在课堂上学习英语的同时，结合课内和课外的语言环境自然习得英语，最终达到熟练运用英语进行交际的目的。为了创建一个良好的英语语言环境，保证充足的语言输入量与输出量，该模式强调要将课内教学与课外学习有机结合起来，强调即学即用、学用结合，强调英语学习的生活化、日常化、内涵化、情景化、趣味化。英力克英语习得模式的研究与实践历时20年，经过师生们的不断创新，已经日趋成熟，并取得了丰硕的成果。

第二，本教材针对的是英语口语教学。本教材的体系是根据英力克英语口语课程的教学环节和步骤设计的，是英力克英语习得模式基本理念的集中体现。英力克英语口语课程有三个重要的环节，这些环节缺一不可：第一个是英语日的 Routine English Communication，即每周四全天，要求学生之间、学生与英语教师之间用英语进行日常交流；第二个是 English Chat，即由学生针对所学演讲的问题进行小组讨论；第三个是 EANLIC Party，即由"学生教师"结合所学演讲的主题，在英语教师的指导下备好课，并用英文举办一场丰富多彩的 EANLIC Party。

第三，本教材体现了 CBI（Content-based Instruction）的教学理念。与传统

的外语教学不同，CBI 强调的是语言所传达的内容和意义，而非语言点的学习和语言技能本身的机械训练。也就是说，CBI 突出外语的工具性特点，强调语言学习的综合性和整体性，强调通过实际运用外语的过程习得语言能力。因此，虽然这门课程是英语口语，却远不止口语训练本身，它涉及了听、说、读、写、译等各方面的综合学习，涉及了中西方文化的对比、跨文化交际意识的培养和提升，以及与演讲主题相关的背景知识。

第四，本教材所支撑的课程体现了翻转课堂（Flipped Classroom）的教学特点。由于学习内容非常丰富，而课堂上英语教师可直接支配的时间又极其有限，因此学生在课前和课后须完成大量的自学任务，提前认真观看演讲视频（至少3~4遍），并了解该演讲的框架、内容，理解相关词句，完成相应的课前学习任务，否则教学效果就会大打折扣，影响英语教师正常开展教学。英语教师上课时主要检验学生学习的效果，解决疑难问题，引导学生深入思考，并督促学生完成相关的学习任务。

第五，本教材所支撑的课程教学充分体现了"以学生为中心"（Student-centered Teaching）的教学理念。即课程教学过程的主角是学生而非英语教师。不论是英语日的 Routine English Communication、English Chat，还是 EANLIC Party，都是由学生唱主角，英语教师扮演评价者（assessor）、助手（assistant）、观察者（observer）和参与者（participant）的角色。

二、编写体系和教学建议

本教材共有 18 个单元，全部选自 TED talks，题材广泛，每个单元都有"Learning Objectives""Text"" Section Ⅰ Pre-class Tasks"" Section Ⅱ Language Focus"" Section Ⅲ Outline of the Speech"" Section Ⅳ Public Speaking Skills""Section Ⅴ English Chat Tasks""Section Ⅵ EANLIC Party Tasks"和"Section Ⅶ Assignment"等几个部分。现将师生在使用本教材时需要注意的事项分述如下。

1. Section Ⅰ　Pre-class Tasks

TED talks 的演讲者大多以英语为母语，常常会有一些专业术语掺杂其中，因此具有一定的语言难度。但由于本教材所选取的演讲视频并不长，学生完全有时间提前观看并及时解决问题。这一点很重要，否则后面的教学将很难正常进行。观看英语演讲视频和模仿英语演讲为学生提供了一种接近真实英语语言应用的环境，对于提高学生的英语语感和语言综合运用能力意义非凡。第一、第二遍以理解演讲内容为主，第三、第四遍则要特别关注演讲者的演讲技巧和演讲中的语言细节。

这个部分给学生提供了有关该演讲的 5 个问题，要求学生通过观看演讲视频和理解演讲内容后，学会脱稿回答，另外还需要学生再设计 5 个开放式问题，并确保能进行流利的脱稿回答。

2. Section Ⅱ　Language Focus

这个部分除将学生在学习该演讲内容时可能碰到的生词和表达列了出来，并提供了国际音标和中英文解释外，还列出了演讲中出现的一些需要进一步理解和消化的句子。为了确保理解正确，要求学生能够准确地翻译这些句子。

3. Section Ⅲ　Outline of the Speech

这个部分以思维导图的形式将本单元演讲的要点展示给学生。教师可以鼓励学生根据自己的理解，创造性地绘出自己的思维导图。

4. Section Ⅳ　Public Speaking Skills

为提高学生的演讲能力和技巧，每个单元都有演讲技巧方面的理论学习内容，英语教师可以结合该单元的演讲原文，根据学生在演讲训练过程中存在的问题，进行有针对性的辅导。

5. Section Ⅴ　English Chat Tasks

English Chat 一般都是在室外或其他相对轻松的环境下进行的小组讨论，形式上类似于传统的 English Corner，但又不是 English Corner。整个讨论和交流过程都须在英语教师的组织下开展，并且遵循两个原则：一是讨论的内容须涉及所学英语演讲的主题内容。在各小组讨论的过程中，英语教师可以深入各个小组检查和评估学生的讨论效果，也可以组织各小组，乃至各班级相互进行交叉检查和交流，最后再汇总情况。二是 English Chat 作为教学环节的一个有机组成部分，英语教师须严格把控其时间、节奏，保证学生英语口语训练的效率，有效避免传统 English Corner 的松散性和不可持续性问题。

在这个教学环节，交谈的内容除课前准备的 5 个问题外，还有针对该英语演讲的结构所进行的讨论。当然，如果时间允许，学生还可以根据时事和其他大家感兴趣的内容进行交流，前提是必须使用英文。

6. Section Ⅵ　EANLIC Party Tasks

EANLIC Party 同样属于教学环节中的一个必要组成部分，但是须在英语教师的指导下，由"学生教师"精心准备教案和 PPT，经英语教师审核通过后，以小组形式轮流，全程用英文组织开展。其组织形式和内容安排相对灵活，可以在达成教学目标任务的前提下充分发挥"学生教师"的创造力，做到教育性、开放性和趣味性相统一，但须有2~3名学生提前准备好演讲内容。演讲结束后，其他学生则对演讲者准备是否充分、声音是否足够大、是否与听众有目光交流、演讲的逻辑是否清晰、支撑论点的论据是否充足等方面进行评价，同时帮助演讲者纠正在英语语音和语法方面出现的问题，并提出建议。

在派对上，师生还应完成所建议的 Debate 话题，其他内容则根据时间灵活安排。在派对结束之前，还应该留出 15 分钟左右的时间，让英语教师进行教学总结和安排相关的课后任务，让学生针对全天的 Routine English Communication 情况开展自评（或互评）。

7. Section Ⅶ　Assignment

这个部分作为课后的教学延伸，要求学生根据任务要求在课后完成，有利于学生对有关知识的巩固和延伸。

总之，本教材的编写遵循了先进的理念，并采用了科学的编写体系，只要采用适合的教学模式和教学方法，相信英语教师和学生定能有所悟、有所得！

最后还要诚挚地感谢丽江师范高等专科学校外国语学院聘请的华东师范大学朱晓映名誉院长和花蓉学术院长对本教材给予的高屋建瓴、耐心、细致的指导和帮助！

段平华

Unit 1	Grit: The Power of Passion and Perseverance	/ 1
Unit 2	The Power of Believing That You Can Improve	/ 10
Unit 3	What the World Can Learn from China's Innovation Playbook	/ 20
Unit 4	How to Triple Your Memory by Using This Trick	/ 32
Unit 5	The Generation That's Remaking China	/ 43
Unit 6	Why 30 Is Not the New 20	/ 55
Unit 7	How China Is Changing the Future of Shopping	/ 67
Unit 8	Every Kid Needs a Champion	/ 78
Unit 9	How Bees Can Keep the Peace Between Elephants and Humans	/ 87
Unit 10	The Brain Changing Benefits of Exercise	/ 99
Unit 11	What Makes a Good Life	/ 111
Unit 12	10 Ways to Have a Better Conversation	/ 121

Unit 13	Living Beyond Limits	/ 132
Unit 14	How to Gain Control of Your Free Time	/ 141
Unit 15	How AI Could Save (Not Destroy) Education	/ 152
Unit 16	Learning a Language? Speak It Like You're Playing a Video Game	/ 165
Unit 17	I Am Not Your Asian Stereotype	/ 176
Unit 18	How Societies Can Grow Old Better	/ 186

参考文献 / 199

Unit 1   Grit: The Power of Passion and Perseverance

By Angela Lee Duckworth

Learning Objectives

1. Achieve a thorough understanding of the speech contextually and linguistically.
2. Improve the ability to communicate with others about grit.
3. Understand the different types of speeches.
4. Recognize how essential perseverance is.

Text

When I was 27 years old, I left a very demanding job in management consulting for a job that was even more demanding: teaching. I went to teach seventh graders math in the New York City public schools. And like any teacher, I made quizzes and tests. I gave out homework assignments. When the work came back, I calculated grades.

What struck me was that I.Q. was not the only difference between my best and my worst students. Some of my strongest performers did not have stratospheric I.Q. scores. Some of my smartest kids weren't doing so well.

And that got me thinking. The kinds of things you need to learn in seventh grade math, sure, they're hard: ratios, decimals, the area of a parallelogram. But these concepts are not impossible, and *I was firmly convinced that every one of my students could learn the material if they worked hard and long enough.*

After several more years of teaching, I came to the conclusion that *what we need in education is a much better understanding of students and learning from a motivational perspective, from a psychological perspective.* In education, the one thing we know how to measure best is I.Q., but what if doing well in school and in life depends on much more than your ability to learn quickly and easily?

So I left the classroom, and I went to graduate school to become a psychologist. I started *studying kids and adults in all kinds of super challenging settings, and in every study my question was, who is successful here and why?* My research team and I went to West Point Military Academy. We tried to predict which cadets would stay in military training and which would drop out. We went to the National Spelling Bee and tried to predict which children would advance farthest in competition. We studied rookie teachers working in really tough neighborhoods, asking which teachers are still going to be here in teaching by the end of the school year, and of those, who will be the most effective at improving learning outcomes for their students? We partnered with private companies, asking which of these salespeople is going to keep their jobs? And who's going to earn the most money? *In all those very different contexts, one characteristic emerged as a significant predictor of success.* And it wasn't social intelligence. It wasn't good looks, physical health, and it wasn't I.Q. *It was grit.*

Grit is passion and perseverance for very long-term goals. Grit is having stamina. Grit is sticking with your future, day in, day out, not just for the week, not just for the month, but for years, and working really hard to make that future a reality. Grit is living a life like it's a marathon, not a sprint.

A few years ago, I started studying grit in the Chicago public schools. I asked thousands of high school juniors to take grit questionnaires, and then waited around more than a year to see who would graduate. Turns out that grittier kids were significantly more likely to graduate, even when I matched them on every characteristic I could measure, things like family income, standardized achievement test scores, even how safe kids felt when they were at school. So it's not just at West Point or the National Spelling Bee that grit matters. It's also in school, especially for kids at risk for dropping out. To me, the most shocking thing about grit is how little we know, how little science knows, about building it. Every day, parents and teachers ask me, "How do I build grit in kids? What should I do to teach kids a solid work ethic? How do I keep them motivated for the long run?" The honest answer is, I don't know. What I do know is that *talent doesn't make you gritty.* Our data show very clearly that there are many talented individuals who simply do not follow through on their commitments. In fact, in our data, grit is usually unrelated or even inversely related to measures of talent.

So far, the best idea I've heard about building grit in kids is something called "growth mindset". This is an idea developed at Stanford University by Carol Dweck, and it is the belief that the ability to learn is not fixed and it can change with your effort. Dr.

Dweck has shown that when kids read and learn about the brain and how it changes and grows in response to challenge, they're much more likely to persevere when they fail, because *they don't believe that failure is a permanent condition.*

So "growth mindset" is a great idea for building grit. But we need more. And that's where I'm going to end my remarks, because that's where we are. That's the work that stands before us. We need to take our best ideas, our strongest intuitions, and we need to test them. We need to measure whether we've been successful, and *we have to be willing to fail, to be wrong, to start over again with lessons learned.*

In other words, *we need to be gritty about getting our kids grittier.*

Thank you.

Section I Pre-class Tasks

Directions: *Finish the following tasks before class.*

1. Watch and listen to the speech for the first time, and get the main idea of the speech.

2. Watch the speech for the second time and find the answers to the following questions.

(1) According to Angela Duckworth, what is grit? How to build grit?

(2) According to Angela Duckworth, what struck her most when she was teaching at New York City public schools?

(3) What was the lesson she learned from her teaching experiences?

(4) Can you think of other ways to build grit?

(5) What type of speech is this?

3. Design 5 open-ended questions to interview five other students at the English chat. Write down your questions and peer evaluation in Table 1.1.

Table 1.1 Questions and Peer Evaluation (1)

Questions	Peer Evaluation (appropriateness, grammatical accuracy)
1.	
2.	
3.	
4.	

continued

Questions	Peer Evaluation (appropriateness, grammatical accuracy)
5.	
Student evaluator signature	

Section II Language Focus

1. Words & Expressions

- **grit** /ɡrɪt/ *n.* informal determination to succeed, even in very difficult situations 毅力，勇气

- **perseverance** /ˌpɜːsɪˈvɪərəns/ *n.* the quality of continuing to try to achieve a particular aim despite difficulties 毅力，韧劲，不屈不挠的精神

- **stratospheric** /ˌstrætəˈsferɪk/ *adj.* at or to an extremely high level 在（到）极高水平的

- **ratios** /ˈreɪʃɪəʊz/ *n.* a relationship between two things expressed by two numbers or amounts 比例，比率

- **decimal** /ˈdesɪməl/ *n.* a number in a system based on the number ten that consists of numbers on either side of a decimal point, 0.5, 25.75, and 873.4 are all decimals 小数

- **parallelogram** /ˌpærəˈleləɡræm/ *n.* a shape with four straight sides in which opposite sides are of equal length and are parallel to each other 平行四边形

- **perspective** /pəˈspektɪv/ *n.* a particular attitude towards sth.; a way of thinking about sth. 态度；观点；思考方法

- **psychologist** /saɪˈkɒlədʒɪst/ *n.* a scientist who studies and is trained in psychology; a clinical psychologist (one who treats people with mental disorders of problems) 心理学家；心理学研究者；心理医生

- **West Point Military Academy** 西点军校

- **drop out** 退学；辍学

- **National Spelling Bee** 全国拼字比赛；全美拼字大赛

- **rookie** /ˈrʊki/ *n.* a person who has just started a job or an activity and has very little experience 新手，生手；新队员

- **characteristic** /ˌkærəktəˈrɪstɪk/ *n.* a typical feature of quality that sth./sb. has 特征；特点；品质

- **predictor** /prɪˈdɪktə(r)/ *n.* sth. that can show what will happen in the future 预测器；预示物
- **stamina** /ˈstæmɪnə/ *n.* the physical or mental strength that enables people to do sth. difficult for long periods of time 耐力；耐性；持久力
- **sprint** /sprɪnt/ *n.* a race in which people taking part run, swim, etc. very fast over a short distance 短跑比赛；短距离速度竞赛
- **gritty** /ˈɡrɪti/ *adj.* showing the courage and determination to continue doing sth. difficult or unpleasant 有勇气的；坚定的；坚毅的
- **commitment** /kəˈmɪtmənt/ *n.* a promise to do sth. or to behave in a particular way 承诺；许诺；保证
- **inversely** /ˌɪnˈvɜːsli/ *adv.* oppositely in amount or position to sth. else（数量、位置）相反地；反向地
- **mindset** /ˈmaɪndset/ *n.* a set of attitudes or fixed ideas that sb. has and that are often difficult to change 观念模式;思维倾向;思维模式

2. Sentences for Further Understanding

Directions：*Translate the following sentences from English into Chinese.*

- What struck me was that I.Q. was not the only difference between my best and my worst students.
- I was firmly convinced that every one of my students could learn the material if they worked hard and long enough.
- After several more years of teaching, I came to the conclusion that what we need in education is a much better understanding of students and learning from a motivational perspective, from a psychological perspective.
- We studied rookie teachers working in really tough neighborhoods, asking which teachers are still going to be here in teaching by the end of the school year, and of those, who will be the most effective at improving learning outcomes for their students?
- In all those very different contexts, one characteristic emerged as a significant predictor of success. And it wasn't social intelligence. It wasn't good looks, physical health, and it wasn't I.Q. It was grit.
- Grit is passion and perseverance for very long-term goals.
- Grit is having stamina.
- Grit is sticking with your future, day in, day out, not just for the week, not just for

the month, but for years, and working really hard to make that future a reality.
- Grit is living a life like it's a marathon, not a sprint.
- To me, the most shocking thing about grit is how little we know, how little science knows, about building it.
- What I do know is that talent doesn't make you gritty.
- So far, the best idea I've heard about building grit in kids is something called "growth mindset".
- It is the belief that the ability to learn is not fixed and it can change with your effort.
- They don't believe that failure is a permanent condition.
- We need to measure whether we've been successful, and we have to be willing to fail, to be wrong, to start over again with lessons learned.
- In other words, we need to be gritty about getting our kids grittier.

Section III Outline of the Speech

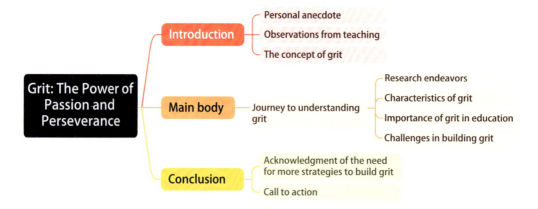

Section IV Public Speaking Skills

There are various types of speeches, each serving a different purpose and catering to different audiences. Here are some common types of speeches.

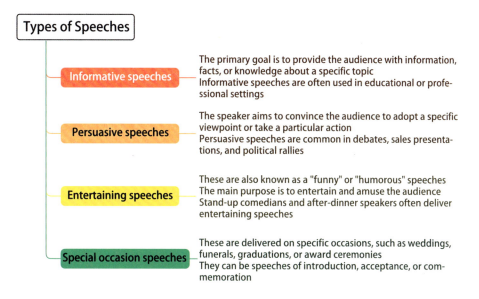

Section V English Chat Tasks

1. Q&A (5 questions): Work in groups to ask and answer questions prepared in the pre-class task.

2. A complete speech includes an introduction, main body and conclusion (Table 1.2). There are many techniques a speaker can use to create these parts of a speech. Discuss in groups what specific techniques the speaker uses in this speech and write down your answers.

Table 1. 2　Sections and Techniques in the Speech(1)

Sections of a Speech	Techniques Used in a Speech	Techniques the Speaker Uses in the Speech
Introduction	1. Relate the topic to the audience 2. State the importance of your topic 3. Startle the audience 4. Arouse the curiosity of the audience 5. Question the audience 6. Begin with a quotation 7. Tell a story	
Main body	1. Evidence and examples 2. Explanation and analysis 3. Visual aids 4. Personal stories or anecdotes 5. Expert opinions or quotes 6. Transitions	

continued

Sections of a Speech	Techniques Used in a Speech	Techniques the Speaker Uses in the Speech
Conclusion	1. Signal the end of the speech 2. Summarize the speech 3. End with a quotation 4. Make a dramatic statement 5. Refer to the introduction	

Section VI EANLIC Party Tasks

1. Group Work

In groups, research an inspirational role model honored in annual Touching China Awards and deliver a speech about their life and achievements.

2. Prepared Speech

Three students will deliver prepared speeches each week. Score their work according to the feedback checklist below (Table 1.3).

Table 1.3   Checklist(1)

Checklist	Speech 1 1–5 From the least to the most	Speech 2 1–5 From the least to the most	Speech 3 1–5 From the least to the most
Is the speech well-prepared?	1 2 3 4 5	1 2 3 4 5	1 2 3 4 5
Was the speaker's voice loud enough?	1 2 3 4 5	1 2 3 4 5	1 2 3 4 5
Did the speaker look at the audience?	1 2 3 4 5	1 2 3 4 5	1 2 3 4 5
Did the speaker look confident?	1 2 3 4 5	1 2 3 4 5	1 2 3 4 5
Was there a clear and logical structure in the speech?	1 2 3 4 5	1 2 3 4 5	1 2 3 4 5
Were all the major claims supported by evidence?	1 2 3 4 5	1 2 3 4 5	1 2 3 4 5
Have you found any mistakes in grammar/pronunciation?			
Do you have any suggestions for the speaker to improve next time?			

3. Debate

Directions: *Work in groups to prepare a claim or counterclaim for the following idea beforehand, and then participate in the debate at the EANLIC Party.*

Some people believe that the key to success is opportunity, while others believe that the key to success is perseverance.

4. Activities Focusing on Words and Expressions

Design an activity using words and expressions from the speech.

Section VII Assignment

Tell a story about "A Personal Hero" that addresses the following requirements:

- Share a story about a successful individual, highlighting how he/she exemplifies "grit".
- Offer personal insights on how to cultivate and apply "grit" in your own life.

Ensure that your story is well-expressed and engaging.

Unit 2 The Power of Believing That You Can Improve

By Carol Dweck

Learning Objectives

1. Achieve a thorough understanding of the speech contextually and linguistically.
2. Learn to express yourselves freely on the topic of a growth mindset.
3. Be able to write the purpose of a speech.
4. Apply a growth mindset to daily life.

Text

I heard about a high school in Chicago where students had to pass a certain number of courses to graduate, and if they didn't pass a course, they got the grade "*Not Yet*". And I think that is fantastic, because if you get a failing grade, you think, I'm nothing, I'm nowhere. But if you get the grade "Not Yet", *you understand that you're on a learning curve. It gives you a path into the future.*

"Not Yet" also gave me insight into a critical event early in my career, a real turning point. I wanted to see how children coped with challenges and difficulty, so I gave 10-year-olds problems that were slightly too hard for them. Some of them reacted in a shockingly positive way. They said things like, "I love a challenge," or, "You know, I was hoping this would be informative." *They understood that their abilities could be developed.* They had what I call a *growth mindset*. But other students felt it was tragic, catastrophic. From their more *fixed mindset* perspective, their intelligence had been up for judgment, and they failed. Instead of luxuriating in the power of yet, they were gripped in the tyranny of now.

So what do they do next? I'll tell you what they do next. In one study, they told us they would probably cheat the next time instead of studying more if they failed a test. In another study, after a failure, they looked for someone who did worse than they did so they could feel really good about themselves. And in study after study, they have run from difficulty. Scientists measured the electrical activity from the brain as students confronted an error. On the left, you see the fixed-mindset students. There's hardly any activity. They run from the error. They don't engage with it. But on the right, you have the students with the growth mindset, the idea that abilities can be developed. *They engage deeply. Their brain is on fire with yet. They engage deeply. They process the error. They learn from it and they correct it.*

How are we raising our children? Are we raising them for now instead of yet? Are we raising kids who are obsessed with getting As? Are we raising kids who don't know how to dream big dreams? Their biggest goal is getting the next A, or the next test score? And are they carrying this need for constant validation with them into their future lives? Maybe, because employers are coming to me and saying, "We have already raised a generation of young workers who can't get through the day without an award."

So what can we do? How can we build that bridge to yet?

Here are some things we can do. First of all, *we can praise wisely, not praising intelligence or talent.* That has failed. Don't do that anymore. But *praising the process that kids engage in, their effort, their strategies, their focus, their perseverance, and their improvement.* This process praise creates kids who are hardy and resilient.

There are other ways to reward yet. We recently teamed up with game scientists from the University of Washington to create a new online math game that rewarded yet. In this game, students were rewarded for effort, strategies and progress. The usual math game rewards you for getting answers right, right now, but this game rewarded process. And we got more effort, more strategies, more engagement over longer periods of time, and more perseverance when they hit really, really hard problems.

Just the words "yet" or "not yet", we're finding, give kids greater confidence and give them a path into the future that creates greater persistence. And we can actually change students' mindsets. In one study, *we taught them that every time they push out of their comfort zone to learn something new and difficult, the neurons in their brain can form new, stronger connections, and over time, they can get smarter.*

Look what happened: In this study, students who were not taught this growth mindset continued to show declining grades over this difficult school transition, but those who were taught this lesson showed a sharp rebound in their grades. We have shown this now, this kind of improvement, with thousands and thousands of kids, especially struggling students.

So let's talk about *equality*. In our country, there are groups of students who chronically underperform, for example, children in inner cities, or children on Native American reservations. And they've done so poorly for so long that many people think it's inevitable. But *when educators create growth mindset classrooms steeped in yet, equality happens.* And here are just a few examples. In one year, a kindergarten class in Harlem, New York scored in the 95th percentile on the national achievement test. Many of those kids could not hold a pencil when they arrived at school. In one year, fourth-grade students in the South Bronx, way behind, became the number one fourth-grade class in the state of New York on the state math test. In a year, to a year and a half, Native American students in a school on a reservation went from the bottom of their district to the top, and that district included affluent sections of Seattle. *So the Native kids outdid the Microsoft kids.*

This happened because *the meaning of effort and difficulty were transformed. Before, effort and difficulty made them feel dumb, made them feel like giving up, but now, effort and difficulty, that's when their neurons are making new connections, stronger connections. That's when they're getting smarter.*

I received a letter recently from a 13-year-old boy. He said, "Dear Professor Dweck, I appreciate that your writing is based on solid scientific research, and that's why I decided to put it into practice. I put more effort into my schoolwork, into my relationship with my family, and into my relationship with kids at school, and I experienced great improvement in all of those areas. I now realize I've wasted most of my life."

Let's not waste any more lives, because once we know that abilities are capable of such growth, *it becomes a basic human right for children, all children, to live in places that create that growth, to live in places filled with "yet".*

Section I Pre-class Tasks

Directions: *Finish the following tasks before class.*

1. Watch and listen to the speech for the first time, and get the main idea of the speech.

2. Watch the speech for the second time and find the answers to the following

questions.

(1) What does the word "power" mean in the title?

(2) How did children cope with challenges and difficulty in Case 1?

(3) What is a growth mindset? What is a fixed mindset?

(4) What is the purpose of the speech?

(5) How do you apply the growth mindset in your life?

3. Design 5 open-ended questions to interview five other students at the English chat. Write down your questions and peer evaluation in Table 2.1.

Table 2.1 Questions and Peer Evaluation(2)

Questions	Peer Evaluation (appropriateness, grammatical accuracy)
1.	
2.	
3.	
4.	
5.	
Student evaluator signature	

Section II Language Focus

1. Words & Expressions

- **curve** /kɜːv/ *n.* a line or surface that bends gradually; a smooth bend 曲线；弧线；曲面；弯曲

- **insight** /ˈɪnsaɪt/ *n.* the ability to see and understand the truth about people or situations 洞察力；领悟；洞悉；了解

- **critical** /ˈkrɪtɪkl/ *adj.* extremely important because a future situation will be affected by it 极重要的；关键的；至关紧要的

- **informative** /ɪnˈfɔːmətɪv/ *adj.* giving useful information 提供有用信息的；给予知识的

- **catastrophic** /ˌkætəˈstrɒfɪk/ *adj.* (of a natural event) causing many people to suffer

灾难性的

- **fixed mindset**　固定型思维
- **luxuriate** /lʌgˈʒʊərieɪt/　*v.* to enjoy being in a very pleasant, comfortable, or relaxing situation or place 尽情享受
- **grip** /ɡrɪp/　*n.* control or power over sb./sth.（对……的）控制，影响力
- **tyranny** /ˈtɪrəni/　*n.* unfair or cruel use of power or authority 暴虐；专横；苛政；专政
- **validation** /ˌvælɪˈdeɪʃn/　*n.* the act of validating; finding or testing the truth of sth. 确认；批准；生效
- **resilient** /rɪˈzɪliənt/　*adj.* able to feel better quickly after sth. unpleasant such as shock, injury, etc. 可迅速恢复的；有适应力的
- **persistence** /pəˈsɪstəns/　*n.* the fact of continuing to try to do sth. despite difficulties, especially when other people are against you and think that you are being annoying or unreasonable 坚持；锲而不舍
- **neuron** /ˈnjʊərɒn/　*n.* a cell that carries information within the brain and between the brain and other parts of the body; a nerve cell 神经元
- **chronically** /ˈkrɒnɪkli/　*adv.* in a slowly developing and long lasting manner 长期地；慢性地；习惯性地
- **percentile** /pəˈsentaɪl/　*n.* (statistics) any of the 99 numbered points that divide an ordered set of scores into 100 parts, each of which contains one-hundredth of the total 百分位，百分位数
- **affluent** /ˈæfluənt/　*adj.* having a lot of money and a good standard of living 富裕的
- **outdo** /ˌaʊtˈduː/　*v.* to be better than someone else at doing something 优于；凌驾；胜过；打败；制服；超越
- **dumb** /dʌm/　*adj.* (informal) stupid 愚蠢的；傻的；笨的
- **solid** /ˈsɒlɪd/　*adj.* that you can rely on; having a strong basis 可靠的；可信赖的；坚实的

2. Sentences for Further Understanding

Directions: *Translate the following sentences from English into Chinese.*

- I think that is fantastic, because if you get a failing grade, you think, I'm nothing, I'm nowhere. But if you get the grade "Not Yet", you understand that you're on a learning curve. It gives you a path into the future.

- "Not Yet" also gave me insight into a critical event early in my career, a real turning point.
- They understood that their abilities could be developed. They had what I call a growth mindset.
- They engage deeply. Their brain is on fire with yet. They engage deeply. They process the error. They learn from it and they correct it.
- How are we raising our children? Are we raising them for now instead of yet? Are we raising kids who are obsessed with getting As? Are we raising kids who don't know how to dream big dreams?
- But praising the process that kids engage in, their effort, their strategies, their focus, their perseverance, and their improvement. This process praise creates kids who are hardy and resilient.
- And we got more effort, more strategies, more engagement over longer periods of time, and more perseverance when they hit really, really hard problems.
- Just the words "yet" or "not yet", we're finding, give kids greater confidence, and give them a path into the future that creates greater persistence.
- Before, effort and difficulty made them feel dumb, made them feel like giving up, but now, effort and difficulty, that's when their neurons are making new connections, stronger connections. That's when they're getting smarter.
- I appreciate that your writing is based on solid scientific research, and that's why I decided to put it into practice.
- I put more effort into my schoolwork, into my relationship with my family, and into my relationship with kids at school, and I experienced great improvement in all of those areas.
- Let's not waste any more lives, because once we know that abilities are capable of such growth, it becomes a basic human right for children, all children, to live in places that create that growth, to live in places filled with "yet".

Section III Outline of the Speech

The Power of Believing That You Can Improve

- Introduction
  - Introduction the concept of "Not Yet"
  - The impact of "Not Yet" on students' learning and mindset
- Main body
  - The power of "yet"
    - Description of "growth mindset" vs. "fixed mindset"
    - Study findings on students' reactions to challenge
    - Comparison of fixed and growth mindsets in handling failures
  - Strategies for fostering a growth mindset
    - Praise wisely
    - Rewards for effort, strategies and progress
    - Teaching the concept of a growth mindset and neuroplasticity
  - Evidence of success
    - Study results showing improvement in grades with growth mindset interventions
    - Examples of classrooms and schools where a growth mindset fosters equality and success
    - Personal testimony: impact on individuals' lives
- Conclusion
  - Recap of the transformative power of fostering a growth mindset
  - Call to promoting "yet" in educaiton and beyond

Section IV Public Speaking Skills

The purpose of a speech can vary depending on the context, audience, and the goals of the speaker. Generally, the main purposes of a speech can be outlined as follows.

Unit 2
The Power of Believing That You Can Improve

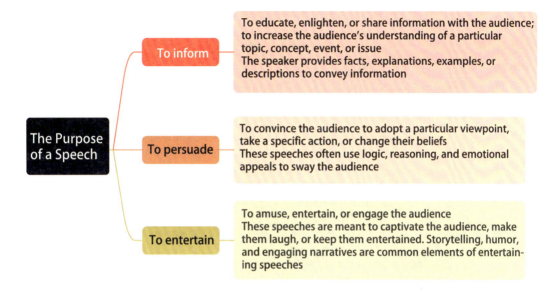

Writing the purpose of a speech is an important step in the speech-writing process. The purpose statement helps you clarify your intentions and guides the content and structure of your speech. Here are some tips to help you write the purpose of a speech effectively.

Section V English Chat Tasks

1. Q&A (5 questions): Work in groups to ask and answer questions prepared in the pre-class task.

2. A complete speech includes an introduction, main body and conclusion (Table 2.2). There are many techniques a speaker can use to create these parts of a speech. Discuss in groups what specific techniques the speaker uses in this speech and write down your answers.

Table 2.2 Sections and Techniques of the Speech (2)

Sections of a Speech	Techniques Used in a Speech	Techniques the Speaker Uses in the Speech
Introduction	1. Relate the topic to the audience 2. State the importance of your topic 3. Startle the audience 4. Arouse the curiosity of the audience 5. Question the audience 6. Begin with a quotation 7. Tell a story	
Main body	1. Evidence and examples 2. Explanation and analysis 3. Visual aids 4. Personal stories or anecdotes 5. Expert opinions or quotes 6. Transitions	
Conclusion	1. Signal the end of the speech 2. Summarize the speech 3. End with a quotation 4. Make a dramatic statement 5. Refer to the introduction	

Section VI EANLIC Party Tasks

1. Group Work

In groups, research an inspirational role model honored in annual Touching China Awards and deliver a speech about their life and achievements.

2. Prepared Speech

Three students will deliver prepared speeches each week. Score their work according to the feedback checklist below (Table 2.3).

Table 2.3 Checklist(2)

Checklist	Speech 1 1-5 From the least to the most	Speech 2 1-5 From the least to the most	Speech 3 1-5 From the least to the most
Is the speech well-prepared?	1 2 3 4 5	1 2 3 4 5	1 2 3 4 5
Was the speaker's voice loud enough?	1 2 3 4 5	1 2 3 4 5	1 2 3 4 5
Did the speaker look at the audience?	1 2 3 4 5	1 2 3 4 5	1 2 3 4 5
Did the speaker look confident?	1 2 3 4 5	1 2 3 4 5	1 2 3 4 5
Was there a clear and logical structure in the speech?	1 2 3 4 5	1 2 3 4 5	1 2 3 4 5
Were all the major claims supported by evidence?	1 2 3 4 5	1 2 3 4 5	1 2 3 4 5
Have you found any mistakes in grammar/pronunciation?			
Do you have any suggestions for the speaker to improve next time?			

3. Debate

Directions: *Work in groups to prepare a claim or counterclaim for the following idea beforehand, and then participate in the debate at the EANLIC Party.*

School should proritize teaching students about growth mindsets over academic content to improve long-term success.

4. Activities Focusing on Words and Expressions

Design an activity using words and expressions from the speech.

Section VII Assignment

Tell a story about your personal growth journey that addresses the following questions:

- What was the most challenging experience you faced while growing up?
- How did you overcome it?
- What did you learn from the experience, or how would you handle it differently if faced with it again today?

Ensure that your story is well-expressed and engaging.

Unit 3 What the World Can Learn from China's Innovation Playbook

By Keyu Jin

Learning Objectives

1. Achieve a thorough understanding of the speech contextually and linguistically.
2. Improve ability to communicate with others about China's innovation.
3. Learn to write the central idea of a speech.
4. Recognize the role of China's innovation in the world.

Text

So when I was born in China in the early 1980s, my country was still a place of scarcity. We lived on rationed food, cooked from communal kitchens and even in Beijing had three nights of blackouts every week. I remember reading poems with my father by candlelight. A special memory from times when Chinese people had little.

And fast forward three decades, China has turned into a country of abundance, especially when it comes to technological power. From high tech to business tech to everyday tech, there isn't anything you can't find, only things you can't imagine. I can buy a can of Coke by scanning my face. A few years ago, I called for toothpaste from my hotel room, and it was delivered to me by a robot. I've seen people live in remote Tibetan mountains blast off cool music with Walkmans powered by solar cells and Chinese solar technology light up homes for African kids who used to study by candlelight, just like me when I was growing up.

So this striking swell of innovation happened even though China remains a developing country, with just a little more than 10,000 dollars of per capita GDP. *So today I want to offer you a different lens to look through, one that shows a unique model that has fostered innovation and technological growth.*

Now the system is far from perfect. And like you, I worry about the rising tensions of a tech race and beyond. But I also believe that, as in any relationship, *a better understanding of each other is going to help us more likely to find common goals to work on rather than a downward spiral that harms all.*

So I'm an economist, *straddling* multiple worlds, as it turns out. One foot in London, where I do my research. And one foot in China, where I spend time with my family and also do a bit of work. And if I had a third foot, it would be in the US, where I was educated. So I can totally see why there's so much misunderstanding and incomprehension about this megacountry that has defiedf conventional wisdom.

So let's start out with how China's innovating. Now, *innovation isn't just about inventing the next new thing*, like the iPhone or 3D printing or sending people to Mars. Technologies that go from zero to one. *It could be new applications, business models, better processes that lower costs.* These one-to-n innovations are just as important. Whatever makes us leaner, cleaner and more productive, all count.

So TikTok might not be the first short-video app, but it has garnered more than a billion users around the world. The Chinese EV company, BYD, didn't make the first *prototype*. But compared to Tesla's price point, the 15,000-dollars EV cabs that I've taken with half a million kilometers of range can meaningfully lead to lower emissions and mass adoption. And in the same way, Chinese mobile phones might not be as revolutionary as iPhone, but in African countries, their market share is well over half.

So this actually solves one big problem for developing countries, which is the lack of access to suitable technologies that they can actually use. And even if China doesn't do many zero-to-one technologies yet—at least not yet—it doesn't mean that it can't master high tech, right? It conducted the first quantum video call, and it launched the first drone that can carry a passenger in air.

So let's go behind the scenes. Now, yes, many of you would say China's got money, markets, talent and troves of data, which is so critical in this information age. But it wasn't just that. *Part of the success was also a "whole nation" approach, or what they call a "juguo" system.* So turning an idea or scientific discovery into commercial success requires an innovation ecosystem. The collaboration of universities, national labs and industries, not to mention enormous amount of funding that covers long and uncertain investment cycles.

Now, many of you might think that groundbreaking technologies are the products of stars, the likes of Steve Jobs or Elon Musks. But every time you use the Internet, the GPS or yell at your Alexa, you have the US government to thank for. We often forget that the Apollo program, the Manhattan Project, even Japan's rise to semiconductor stardom, were all horizontal systems with critical state backing.

Now, *China's "juguo" system is an entire nation behind one strategic goal.* Mobilizing national resources, casting the net wide, not tallying costs. And it's the same system that's used to reap as many Olympic gold medals as possible. And so thanks to this ecosystem, China became the largest consumers and producers of EVs in less than a decade, with more cars sold there than in the rest of the world combined in 2020.

Now in the West, we often talk about "nudging" consumers to make better choices. But in China, mass adoption of next-gen transportation happened like that. Well, in part thanks to the state rolling out four million charging stations around the country, coordinating supply chains from battery makers to control systems and manufacturers. Today, there are 140,000 chargers in the US in the entire country.

So that is kind of, the "whole nation" approach. But that's not actually the story I want to tell you. *There's an even more nuanced story that happens on the ground. We call it the "mayor economy", and it's a decentralized economic model that galvanizes creativity from the ground up.* And contrary to popular perception, it isn't a centralized approach dominated by an almighty state.

And so here's how it works. So Nio is one of the top three EV companies in China. Its cars are driven everywhere on the streets of Beijing and Shanghai. Now, two years after it was listed on Nasdaq in 2018, it was on the verge of bankruptcy. Now, at this point, the local government of Hefei, a small town in eastern China with five million people, convinced it to move its headquarters there. The local government *injected* a billion dollars in exchange for a 25-percent stake, arranged more loans for the company and most importantly, organized an entire supply chain around Nio. It took only a year before Nio's production grew by 81 percent, and its market cap went from four to 100 billion dollars. And the local government of Hefei cashed out within a year, and Nio's life was saved.

And so for every local government behind a Nio, there's another mayor behind a competitor. And there are literally hundreds of EV companies vying for survival in ruthless competition. So, if you are actually a promising tech company, local governments will move mountains to help. Remove red tape, check. Find you more financing, check. Get a job for your spouse, check. Piece of cake. They are a one-stop shop, as they like to call themselves. Now in the vigorous bid for Amazon's second headquarters, there were some creative offers. One state sent a giant cactus as a gift. Another state offered to rename a town Amazon. But it basically came to some tax breaks, not quite like what the Chinese mayors had to offer.

But of course, the US government is no stranger to supporting big-shot companies like SpaceX and Tesla, offering billions in benefits. But in China, it's really this marriage between hyper-charged local officials and intrepid entrepreneurs of all ilk that is at the heart of its model. And here's why. So the local government of Hefei, the one that made a killing with Nio, well, it wasn't just after the return on investment, per se. But it was by luring companies like Nio that it's looking to create a mini Silicon Valley of sorts. An industrial clutter, a talent pool, a flourishing retail and service industry that gets them more jobs, more tax revenues. And guess what? Even the real estate and land they own are suddenly worth more, all because of the economics of agglomeration and multiplier effects, because the local mayors are actually an equity stakeholder of the entire city.

So in sum, it's this political centralization and economic decentralization that is actually a simple representation of China's model. It's the same model used to urbanize, to grow and now to innovate.

Now, for all of its successes, there were huge costs, I admit. Waste left in the wake, inefficient investments, wrong bets. Now, some of these challenges are being addressed, thankfully, like environmental degradation, but there are others that remain in urgent need of fixing. So I'm not suggesting that there's some universal recipe or that it's perfect or that it can be easily replicated. But what we do know is that there's more than one way of making things work. And recognizing that there is some wisdom to China's approach doesn't mean endorsing all of it. But I guess there's something to learn from each other. And for one, China didn't sit on the tarmac waiting for a technological takeoff. Instead, it was the big push from the ground up.

So I came to the US as an exchange student in 1997, and I was mesmerized. I saw enormous possibility between the East and the West, as they competed, collaborated and spurred each other forward. I still believe in this, even though frost has set in and there may be chill in the air for some time between the two largest economies in the world. Some may fear China's juggernaut innovation. Some may not like competition, which is rarely comfortable. But having someone in your rearview mirror helps you keep up the pace.

Japan's technological rise in the 1980s pushed the US to overhaul its innovation system and regain the lead in the 1990s. The US subsequently did the same for Japan, and as a result, we all have cheaper and better products. Today, Chinese EV company BYD is pushing Tesla to new heights and vice versa. Tesla opted for a Chinese battery maker, which is pushing the German government to do more in that space. And it's that mutual learning and constant threat of being overtaken that pushes the technology frontier further and beyond. But one thing's for sure, true, it just doesn't happen in geographical isolation.

So ... I've come here, and I imagine the possibilities between the two countries, and I understand that there are national security concerns that countries will have to respect. But not everything is about national security. The trillion dollars or more at stake with the economic *disengagement* between the two largest countries can do so much as eradicate malaria, end world hunger, conserve biodiversity and more. *So let's not forget that there are more sacred things in life.* Such as a brighter future for our children and a cleaner Earth. *Let's not forget that in the developing world, there's still so much unnecessary misery. And that its people also have the right to enjoy the dignity in life as those who are more fortunate.*

And so for all of this to happen, it seems to me that *what we ultimately need is the cheapest and best technologies, rather than worry about where they come from or who will dominate.*

Thanks.

Section I Pre-class Tasks

Directions: *Finish the following tasks before class.*

1. Watch and listen to the speech for the first time, and get the main idea of the speech.

2. Watch the speech for the second time and find the answers to the following questions.

(1) According to the speaker, what is innovation?

(2) What is the China's "whole nation" approach?

(3) What is the enormous possibility between the East and the West according to the speaker?

(4) What is the central idea of the speech?

(5) What can the world learn from China's innovation playbook?

3. Design 5 open-ended questions to interview five other students at the English chat. Write down your questions and peer evaluation in Table 3.1.

Table 3.1 Questions and Peer Evaluation (3)

Questions	Peer Evaluation (appropriateness, grammatical accuracy)
1.	
2.	
3.	
4.	
5.	
Student evaluator signature	

Section II Language Focus

1. Words & Expressions

- **scarcity** /ˈskeəsəti/ *n.* if there is a scarcity of sth., there is not enough of it and it is difficult to obtain it 缺乏；不足；稀少

- **ration** /ˈræʃn/ *v.* to limit sb./sth. to a fixed amount of sth. 配给；定量供应；限定……的量

- **innovation** /ˌɪnəˈveɪʃn/ *n.* the introduction of new things, ideas or ways of doing sth. 创新；改革；(新事物、思想或方法的) 创造；新方法；新思想

- **straddle** /ˈstrædl/ *v.* if sth. straddles a river, road, border, or other places, it stretches across it or exists on both sides of it 横跨，同属 (不同时期、活动或群体)；跨过，横跨 (河流、道路或一片土地)

- **mega** /ˈmegə/ *adj.* very large or impressive 巨大的；极佳的

- **prototype** /ˈprəʊtətaɪp/ *n.* the first design of sth. from which other forms are copied or developed 原型；雏形；最初形态

- **groundbreaking** /ˈgraʊndbreɪkɪŋ/ *adj.* making new discoveries; using new methods 开创性的；突破性的

- **semiconductor** /ˌsemikənˈdʌktə(r)/ *n.* a solid substance that conducts electricity in particular conditions, better than insulators but not as well as conductors 半导体

- **galvanize** /ˈgælvənaɪz/ *v.* to galvanize someone means to cause them to take action, for example, by making them feel very excited, afraid, or angry 使振奋；使震惊

- **inject** /ɪnˈdʒekt/　*v.* to give money to an organization, a project, etc. so that it can function（给……）投入（资金）
- **vie** /vaɪ/　*v.* to compete strongly with sb. in order to obtain or achieve sth. 激烈竞争；争夺
- **revenue** /ˈrevənjuː/　*n.* the money that a government receives from taxes or that an organization, etc. receives from its business 财政收入；税收收入；收益
- **agglomeration** /əˌɡlɒməˈreɪʃn/　*n.* a group of things put together in no particular order or arrangement 集聚；聚集；（杂乱聚集的）团，块，堆
- **stakeholder** /ˈsteɪkhəʊldə(r)/　*n.* a person or company that is involved in a particular organization, project, system, etc., especially because they have invested money in it（某组织、工程、体系等的）参与人，参与方；有权益关系者
- **degradation** /ˌdeɡrəˈdeɪʃn/　*n.* the process of sth. being damaged or made worse 毁坏；恶化（过程）
- **replicate** /ˈreplɪkeɪt/　*v.* to copy sth. exactly 复制；（精确地）仿制
- **endorse** /ɪnˈdɔːs/　*v.* to say publicly that you support a person, statement or course of action（公开）赞同；支持；认可
- **tarmac** /ˈtɑːmæk/　*n.* a black material used for making road surfaces, that consists of small stones mixed with tar 塔玛克柏油碎石（用作铺筑路面材料）
- **mesmerize** /ˈmezməraɪz/　*v.* to have such a strong effect on you that you cannot give your attention to anything else 迷住；吸引
- **spur** /spɜː(r)/　*v.* a fact or an event that makes you want to do sth. better or more quickly 鞭策；激励；刺激；鼓舞
- **juggernaut** /ˈdʒʌɡənɔːt/　*n.* a large and powerful force or institution that cannot be controlled 无法控制的强大机构；不可抗拒的强大力量
- **overhaul** /ˈəʊvəhɔːl/　*v.* an examination of a machine or system, including doing repairs on it or making changes to it 对……进行彻底革新；全面修订
- **disengagement** /ˌdɪsɪnˈɡeɪdʒmənt/　*n.* the act of releasing from an attachment or connection 脱离；分离

2. Sentences for Further Understanding

Directions: *Translate the following sentences from English into Chinese.*

- So when I was born in China in the early 1980s, my country was still a place of scarcity.

- I remember reading poems with my father by candlelight. A special memory from times when Chinese people had little.
- From high tech to business tech to everyday tech, there isn't anything you can't find, only things you can't imagine.
- But I also believe that, as in any relationship, a better understanding of each other is going to help us more likely to find common goals to work on rather than a downward spiral that harms all.
- Innovation could be new applications, business models, better processes that lower costs.
- And in the same way, Chinese mobile phones might not be as revolutionary as iPhone, but in African countries, their market share is well over half.
- It conducted the first quantum video call, and it launched the first drone that can carry a passenger in air.
- Part of the success was also a "whole nation" approach, or what they call a "juguo" system.
- We call it the "mayor economy", and it's a decentralized economic model that galvanizes creativity from the ground up.
- So in sum, it's this political centralization and economic decentralization that is actually a simple representation of China's model.
- China didn't sit on the tarmac waiting for a technological takeoff. Instead, it was the big push from the ground up.
- I saw enormous possibility between the East and the West, as they competed, collaborated and spurred each other forward.
- But having someone in your rearview mirror helps you keep up the pace.
- And that its people also have the right to enjoy the dignity in life as those who are more fortunate.
- And so for all of this to happen, it seems to me that what we ultimately need is the cheapest and best technologies, rather than worry about where they come from or who will dominate.

Section III Outline of the Speech

Section IV Public Speaking Skills

The central idea of a speech, often referred to as the thesis statement, is a specific and detailed statement that encapsulates the main message or points of the speech. Here are steps on how to write a strong central idea for a speech.

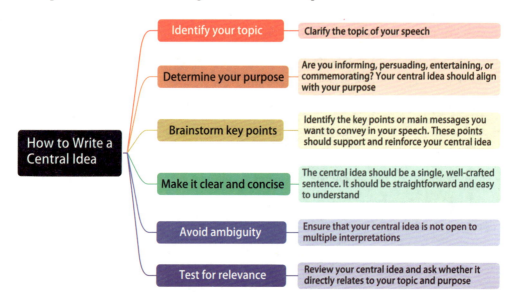

Here's an example of a central idea for a speech on the importance of recycling: Central Idea: "Recycling not only reduces waste but also conserves resources, lowers pollution, and plays a vital role in preserving the environment for future generations."

This central idea is clear, specific, and communicates the key message that the speech will address. It identifies the topic (recycling) and its importance while giving a hint of the main supporting points.

Section V English Chat Tasks

1. Q&A (5 questions): Work in groups to ask and answer questions prepared in the pre-class task.

2. A complete speech includes an introduction, main body and conclusion (Table 3.2). There are many techniques a speaker can use to create these parts of a speech. Discuss in groups what specific techniques the speaker uses in this speech and write down your answers.

Table 3.2 Sections and Techniques of the Speech(3)

Sections of a Speech	Techniques Used in a Speech	Techniques the Speaker Uses in the Speech
Introduction	1. Relate the topic to the audience 2. State the importance of your topic 3. Startle the audience 4. Arouse the curiosity of the audience 5. Question the audience 6. Begin with a quotation 7. Tell a story	
Main body	1. Evidence and examples 2. Explanation and analysis 3. Visual aids 4. Personal stories or anecdotes 5. Expert opinions or quotes 6. Transitions	
Conclusion	1. Signal the end of the speech 2. Summarize the speech 3. End with a quotation 4. Make a dramatic statement 5. Refer to the introduction	

Section VI EANLIC Party Tasks

1. Group Work

In groups, research an inspirational role model honored in annual Touching China Awards and deliver a speech about their life and achievements.

2. Prepared Speech

Three students will deliver prepared speeches each week. Score their work according to the feedback checklist below (Table 3.3).

Table 3.3 Checklist (3)

Checklist	Speech 1 1-5 From the least to the most	Speech 2 1-5 From the least to the most	Speech 3 1-5 From the least to the most
Is the speech well-prepared?	1 2 3 4 5	1 2 3 4 5	1 2 3 4 5
Was the speaker's voice loud enough?	1 2 3 4 5	1 2 3 4 5	1 2 3 4 5
Did the speaker look at the audience?	1 2 3 4 5	1 2 3 4 5	1 2 3 4 5
Was there a clear and logical structure in the speech?	1 2 3 4 5	1 2 3 4 5	1 2 3 4 5
Were all the major claims supported by evidence?	1 2 3 4 5	1 2 3 4 5	1 2 3 4 5
Did the speaker look confident?	1 2 3 4 5	1 2 3 4 5	1 2 3 4 5
Have you found any mistakes in grammar/pronunciation?			
Do you have any suggestions for the speaker to improve next time?			

3. Debate

Directions: *Work in groups to prepare a claim or counterclaim for the following idea beforehand, and then participate in the debate at the EANLIC Party.*

Will international competition accelerate or impede the growth of a nation's strength?

4. Activities Focusing on Words and Expressions

Design an activity using words and expressions from the speech.

Section VII Assignment

Tell a story about "China Speed" based on your personal growth journey. Ensure that your story is well-expressed and engaging.

Unit 4 How to Triple Your Memory by Using This Trick

By Ricardo Lieuw On

Learning Objectives

1. Achieve a thorough understanding of the speech contextually and linguistically.
2. Be able to express yourselves more freely on the topic of memory.
3. Practice utilizing effective speech beginning techniques when delivering a speech.
4. Learn to apply associative memory approach in daily life and develop innovative thinking.

Text

So, I have a little test for you. Don't panic. I'm not here to judge you. It's just a little test, OK? First, you get 30 seconds to memorize 10 words in the right order. After that, you get 30 seconds to write down what you remembered. And then finally, you get 30 seconds to check your answers. So, are you guys ready? Well, we're going to start anyway. So, memorize 10 words in the right order in 30 seconds in three, two, one, go! OK. Stop. Now write down what you remember. OK, and stop. Now quickly check your answers. OK, and stop. Very exciting; I heard a lot of grunting and moaning. So I hope I didn't stress you out too much. Now a moment of reflection. I'd like you to ask yourself, "How did I memorize this, and was it the best way to do it?" Now, for the generation of my parents and grandparents, being able to memorize something like this was an absolutely essential skill. But nowadays, why would anyone want to remember a list of anything? You just take a picture of the screen, and you're done, right? So with all the technology we have these days, it seemed as if memorizing has somehow become less important. So *why should we then, in today's day and age, still want to get better at memorizing*? Well, to answer that question, I'd like to tell you a little story. In high school, I flunked a grade, twice. After seven years of torture, I finally got my diploma. Sweet, sweet freedom! What would I do with it? I didn't know. One thing I did know, however, was that I didn't want to go back to school. Because that old learning business, it wasn't cut out for me. So instead, I went to sunny California for nine months, and there I worked as a bagger, not beggar—bagger. So in a supermarket, I had to put people's groceries in bags, and then I'd get a little tip. Surprisingly, that year I learned so much. I learned how to bag a bunch of groceries really, really quickly. I learned how to drive a car. And in California, people are a little bit more open than they are in Amsterdam. So I also learned how to have a little chat with a stranger, just for the hell of it. That year I discovered that I don't hate learning, just the specific way of doing it. So I decided to go and study psychology. Now for the first time ever, I was getting information that I absolutely wanted to know. Now I was spending more time in the library than I spent skipping school as a teenager, voluntarily. The only problem was that I was spending all of my time in the library because I'd never learned how to learn. So I started experimenting with different methods of reading texts, of memorizing texts, and I got my reading time of three hours per chapter down to one. This way of studying enabled me to do an honors program, to get my degree, and to fall in love with learning. And now I happily work for a company called Remind, in which we teach people the science and art of learning. We're trying to bring back into education what we ourselves missed. Now for the past three years, we've also organized the Dutch National Memory Championships for high schoolers. We do this to show *that everybody is capable of amazing feats of memory, but also to show that memorization is about a lot more than just learning your French or your Spanish words.* And today I'd also like to share this with you. So, in the beginning, *I made you do this little test, just to make you aware of how you're memorizing things right now.* Next, *I'd like to give you a new type of memory experience.* This time you can even sit back and relax. So I'm going to ask you to find a comfortable position to sit, to close your eyes, and to take a deep breath. Now, I want you to think of someone you know called John, and I want you to see him. Now, John just grabbed the sun out of the sky, and he just threw it on your feet. And now your feet are getting really big and red and swollen because John just threw the sun on your feet. Now you look to your knees, and on your knees, you see 10 little guys playing basketball—very strange sight. And on their shirts, you can see in brightly colored letters the "New York Knicks", so you have some Knicks on your knees. Next, you look to where your thighs are, but they're gone. Your thighs have been replaced with Fords, the cars. They could be Ford Focuses or Ford Mustangs. Now, with your bottom, you feel a hard plastic seat of a go-kart vibrating. With your bottom, you feel the hard plastic seat of a go-kart. Your belly starts rumbling very loudly. So you follow your belly, and it leads you to McDonald's, and there Ronald McDonald starts shooting rays of light at you with a ray gun.

Ronald McDonald is shooting rays of light at you with a ray gun. He hits you on your chest, and now from your chest, a big bush of gray hairs is growing. A huge bush of gray hair is growing from your chest. So obviously, you hurry home to shave it off, and on your doormat, you see a letter. So you open it and it has good news. As you read it, you feel a huge weight falling off your shoulders. A huge weight falling off your shoulders. Your shoulders get all light and tingly because you just paid all of your bills. Big bills, little bills, each and every bill has been paid for, and you have plenty of money to spare. Now you proceed to the bathroom, because now on your neck, a bunch of tiny bushes of thin blonde hairs have appeared. On your neck, a bunch of tiny bushes of thin blonde hair. As you look in the mirror, suddenly your mouth just starts talking all by itself, and it's saying, "Yes, we can; yes, we can; yes, we can." Now you turn around, and now suddenly your eyes are, ah, because Donald Duck just poked out both of your eyes with a trumpet made of pure gold. Now you can open your eyes again and come back to this place. Luckily, it's a lot safer here than where you just came from.

So, I just made you guys memorize the past 10 presidents of the United States of America in the right order. Now I'm going to show you, and then you can see how many of these you still know. So with each body part, I'm going to ask you what happened there, and then you could think of it. Even better would be if you just shout it out. Now, what happened to your feet?

John threw the sun, yeah—President Johnson. Now, what happened on your knees? Knicks, yes—President Nixon. OK. So what were your thighs replaced with? Fords—President Ford. OK, and what did you feel with your bottom? OK, President Carter, yes. Some people are ahead of the game. Now, your belly led you to McDonald's; what happened? OK. Ronald McDonald shooting rays of … So Ronald Reagan. He hits in your chest, and you got what? Big bush of gray hairs—Bush Senior.

Now, your shoulders got light, why? Paid all your bills—Bill Clinton. Now, what did you have on your neck? OK, a bush of thin blonde hairs. Bush Junior. What was your mouth saying? "Yes we can"—President Obama. And what happened to your eyes? Yeah, Donald Duck, trumpet, pure gold. Who else but Donald Trump? So, if you memorized more this time than the first time, please stand up. OK. So we have almost everyone standing up; that's awesome. Now, if you think this way of memorizing is more fun than the last way you used, please stand up or remain standing if you're already standing. Oh whoa, now we almost have everyone. I'm very pleased to see this. OK. You guys can sit back down. Thank you very much. Now, *when you make bizarre images to memorize, suddenly it becomes a lot easier.*

If you tie these bizarre images to a place you know well, like your body, suddenly memorizing things in order becomes a lot easier. OK. Well, cool. But I asked you guys in the beginning, "Why should we, in today's day and age, still want to get better at this— at memorizing?" Well, because *by getting better in a skill like this, you can also get better at a different skill; the skill of experimentation.* By experimenting with different methods of doing things, I found out that I can get better at anything. I found out what works for me and what doesn't. What if I'd never learned the skill of experimentation? I may have never gone back to school; I may have never enjoyed studying psychology, and I probably would not have been standing here today, because one of the things I thought I really couldn't do was public speaking. Now, there are people of every generation not doing things that they might love, that they might even be great at because they think they can't do it. So how beautiful would it be if in schools we can teach kids that they can get better at anything, and they can even get better at getting better at things, get it? But not just the kids, because the older generation is often seen as too old to learn. But they're not too rusty. Anyone can improve themselves by experimenting, and I hope you experienced that today. Now at Remind, *we break up this process of experimentation into three steps: the check, the experience and the experiment. The check is all about becoming aware of what you're doing right now.* So maybe during the first test, you became aware of the fact that you just repeat the words over and over and that doesn't work too well. The second step: *the experience is all about being open to new possibilities and trying them out.* So maybe during the visualization, you realize that this works a bit better or at least you like it more. And the third step is *the experiment. This is about taking something from that new experience that you had and applying it in your own life to see how it works for you.* So, maybe you're one of those people that when someone introduces themselves to you, you just immediately forget their name. Yeah, sound familiar? And you want to use visualization to do something about that.

So far I've only taken you guys through the first two steps. The final step is up to you. So when I'm done here, I'd like you to take a moment for yourself and to write down an experiment on the little card we've given you and to put that in your wallet as a reminder. By continually following these steps of experimentation, you discover what you're doing; you keep yourself open to new possibilities, and you allow yourself to continually transform. And regardless of what you're learning, be it memorizing or martial arts or mathematics, you'll get better not only in the skill that you're trying to develop, but you'll get better at the process of learning itself. And that's something that sticks. It's something you could take with you to your new job, your new hobby, your new relationship, your new whatever. So this is something absolutely everyone should know, and I believe we should teach it in schools. But let's not just wait for it to be implemented in schools. I also believe that *the most important change starts with the individual. It starts with you. So, go out there and experiment.*

Learn something new or a new way of approaching something old because there are few skills as valuable as the art of learning.

Thank you.

Section I Pre-class Tasks

Directions: *Finish the following tasks before class.*

1. Watch and listen to the speech for the first time, and get the main idea of the speech.

2. Watch the speech for the second time and find the answers to the following questions.

(1) According to the speaker, what kind of tricks did he mention to triple one's memory?

(2) What methods does the speaker use to help the audience remember the names of past 10 presidents of the United States of America?

(3) What are the three steps of experimentation?

(4) What's your understanding of this sentence "Learn something new or a new way of approaching something old because there are few skills as valuable as the art of learning"?

(5) How does the speaker start his speech?

3. Design 5 open-ended questions to interview five other students at the English chat. Write down your questions and peer evaluation in Table 4.1.

Table 4.1　Questions and Peer Evaluation（4）

Questions	Peer Evaluation （appropriateness, grammatical accuracy）
1.	
2.	
3.	
4.	
5.	
Student evaluator signature	

Section II　Language Focus

1. Words & Expressions

- **panic** /ˈpænɪk/　*v.* to suddenly feel frightened so that you cannot think clearly and you say or do sth. stupid, dangerous, etc.; to make sb. do this （使）惊慌；惊慌失措

- **moan** /məʊn/　*v.* to moan means to complain or speak in a way which shows that you are very unhappy 呻吟；抱怨；发牢骚

- **flunk** /flʌŋk/　*v.* to fail an exam, a test or a course 在（考试）中不及格；未通过（某一课程）

- **skip** /skɪp/　*v.* to not do sth. that you usually do or should do 不做（应做的事等）；不参加

- **voluntarily** /ˈvɒləntrəli/　*adv.* willingly; without being forced 自愿地；自动地；主动地

- **grab** /græb/　*v.* to take or hold sb./sth. with your hand suddenly, firmly or roughly 抓住；攫取

- **swollen** /ˈswəʊlən/　*adj.* (of a part of the body) larger than normal, especially as a result of a disease or an injury （身体的一部分）肿胀的；肿起来的

- **thigh** /θaɪ/　*n.* the top parts of your legs between the knee and the hip 大腿；股

- **go-kart** /ˈgəʊ kɑːt/　*n.* a go-kart is a very small motor vehicle with four wheels, used for racing 卡丁车；（无篷无门的）微型赛车

- **vibrate** /vaɪˈbreɪt/　*n.* to move or make sth. move from side to side very quickly and with small movements （使）振动；颤动；摆动

- **rumbling** /ˈrʌmblɪŋ/ *n.* a long deep sound or series of sounds 持续而低沉的声音；隆隆声；辘辘声；咕噜声

- **tingly** /ˈtɪŋgli/ *adj.* if sth. pleasant or exciting makes you feel tingly, it gives you a pleasant warm feeling 舒心的；惬意的；愉悦的

- **trumpet** /ˈtrʌmpɪt/ *n.* a brass musical instrument made of a curved metal tube that you blow into, with three valves for changing the note 小号

- **bizarre** /bɪˈzɑː(r)/ *adj.* very strange or unusual 极其怪诞的；异乎寻常的

- **experimentation** /ɪkˌsperɪmenˈteɪʃn/ *n.* the activity or process of experimenting 实验；试验；尝试

- **visualization** /ˌvɪʒuəlaɪˈzeɪʃn/ *n.* if you visualize sth., you imagine what it is like by forming a mental picture of it 使形象化；想象；设想；可视化

- **approach** /əˈprəʊtʃ/ *v.* when you approach sth., you get closer to it 靠近；走近

2. Sentences for Further Understanding

Directions: *Translate the following sentences from English into Chinese.*

- So I hope I didn't stress you out too much.
- So with all the technology we have these days, it seemed as if memorizing has somehow become less important.
- One thing I did know, however, was that I didn't want to go back to school. Because that old learning business, it wasn't cut out for me.
- Now I was spending more time in the library than I spent skipping school as a teenager, voluntarily.
- We do this to show that everybody is capable of amazing feats of memory, but also to show that memorization is about a lot more than just learning your French or your Spanish words.
- A huge bush of gray hair is growing from your chest.
- As you read it, you feel a huge weight falling off your shoulders.
- Your shoulders get all light and tingly because you just paid all of your bills.
- Donald Duck just poked out both of your eyes with a trumpet made of pure gold.
- Luckily, it's a lot safer here than where you just came from.
- If you memorized more this time than the first time, please stand up.
- If you tie these bizarre images to a place you know well, like your body, suddenly memorizing things in order becomes a lot easier.
- Anyone can improve themselves by experimenting, and I hope you experienced that

today.

- Learn something new or a new way of approaching something old because there are few skills as valuable as the art of learning.

Section III Outline of the Speech

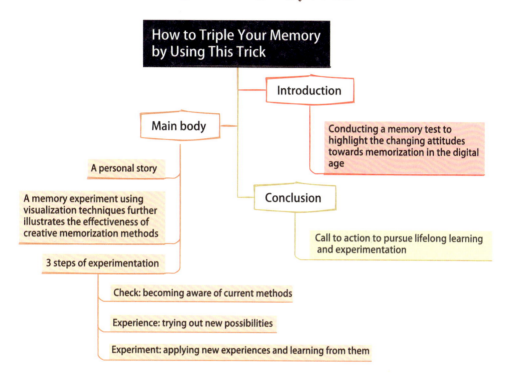

Section IV Public Speaking Skills

Beginning a speech effectively is crucial for capturing your audience's attention and setting the tone for your presentation. Here are some strategies and techniques to start your speech.

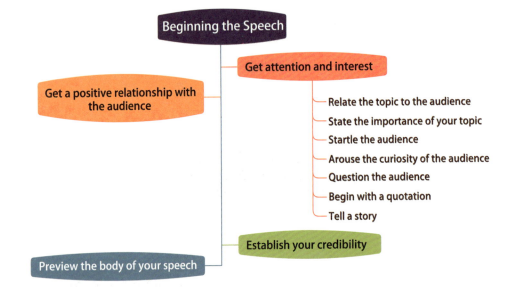

Section V English Chat Tasks

1. Q&A (5 questions): Work in groups to ask and answer questions prepared in the pre-class task.

2. A complete speech includes an introduction, main body and conclusion (Table 4.2). There are many techniques a speaker can use to create these parts of a speech. Discuss in groups what specific techniques the speaker uses in this speech and write down your answers.

Table 4.2 Sections and Techniques of the Speech (4)

Sections of a Speech	Techniques Used in a Speech	Techniques the Speaker Uses in the Speech
Introduction	1. Relate the topic to the audience 2. State the importance of your topic 3. Startle the audience 4. Arouse the curiosity of the audience 5. Question the audience 6. Begin with a quotation 7. Tell a story	
Main body	1. Evidence and examples 2. Explanation and analysis 3. Visual aids 4. Personal stories or anecdotes 5. Expert opinions or quotes 6. Transitions	

continued

Sections of a Speech	Techniques Used in a Speech	Techniques the Speaker Uses in the Speech
Conclusion	1. Signal the end of the speech 2. Summarize the speech 3. End with a quotation 4. Make a dramatic statement 5. Refer to the introduction	

Section VI EANLIC Party Tasks

1. Group Work

In groups, research an inspirational role model honored in annual Touching China Awards and deliver a speech about their life and achievements.

2. Prepared Speech

Three students will deliver prepared speeches each week. Score their work according to the feedback checklist below (Table 4.3).

Table 4.3 Checklist (4)

Checklist	Speech 1 1–5 From the least to the most	Speech 2 1–5 From the least to the most	Speech 3 1–5 From the least to the most
Is the speech well-prepared?	1 2 3 4 5	1 2 3 4 5	1 2 3 4 5
Was the speaker's voice loud enough?	1 2 3 4 5	1 2 3 4 5	1 2 3 4 5
Did the speaker look at the audience?	1 2 3 4 5	1 2 3 4 5	1 2 3 4 5
Did the speaker look confident?	1 2 3 4 5	1 2 3 4 5	1 2 3 4 5
Was there a clear and logical structure in the speech?	1 2 3 4 5	1 2 3 4 5	1 2 3 4 5
Were all the major claims supported by evidence?	1 2 3 4 5	1 2 3 4 5	1 2 3 4 5
Have you found any mistakes in grammar/pronunciation?			
Do you have any suggestions for the speaker to improve next time?			

3. Debate

Directions: *Work in groups to prepare a claim or counterclaim for the following*

idea beforehand, and then participate in the debate at the EANLIC Party.

Some people believe that good memory can be improved by training, while others think that good memory is innate.

4. Activities Focusing on Words and Expressions

Design an activity using words and expressions from the speech.

Section VII Assignment

Figure out a fast and easy way to memorize the following 10 words by using the tricks you have learned from the speech.

1	2	3	4	5	6	7	8	9	10
beard	object	jacket	secret	edge	nothing	date	band	punch	gas

Unit 5 The Generation That's Remaking China

By Yang Lan

Learning Objectives

1. Achieve a thorough understanding of the speech contextually and linguistically.
2. Improve the ability to freely express personal views on the topic of the young generation.
3. Learn to use examples to support main points in a speech.
4. Foster a sense of social responsibility.

Text

The night before I was heading for Scotland, I was invited to host the final of "China's Got Talent" show in Shanghai with the 80,000 live audience in the stadium. Guess who was the performing guest? Susan Boyle. And I told her, "I'm going to Scotland the next day." She sang beautifully, and she even managed to say a few words in Chinese: 送你葱. So it's not like "hello" or "thank you", that ordinary stuff. It means "green onion for free". Why did she say that? Because it was a line from our Chinese parallel Susan Boyle—a 50-some-year-old woman, a vegetable vendor in Shanghai, who loves singing Western opera, but she didn't understand any English or French or Italian, so she managed to fill in the lyrics with vegetable names in Chinese. And the last sentence of Nessun Dorma that she was singing in the stadium was "green onion for free". So [as] Susan Boyle was saying that, 80,000 live audience sang together. That was hilarious.

So I guess both Susan Boyle and this vegetable vendor in Shanghai belonged to otherness. *They were the least expected to be successful in the business called entertainment, yet their courage and talent brought them through. And a show and a platform gave them the stage to realize their dreams.* Well, being different is not that difficult. *We are all different from different perspectives. But I think being different is good, because you present a different point of view. You may have the chance to make a difference.*

My generation has been very fortunate to witness and participate in the historic transformation of China that has made so many changes in the past 20, 30 years. I remember that in the year of 1990, when I was graduating from college, I was applying for a job in the sales department of the first five-star hotel in Beijing, Great Wall Sheraton—it's still there. So after being interrogated by this Japanese manager for half an hour, he finally said, "So, Miss Yang, do you have any questions to ask me?" I summoned my courage and poise and said, "Yes, but could you let me know, what actually do you sell?" I didn't have a clue what a sales department was about in a five-star hotel. That was the first day I set my foot in a five-star hotel.

Around the same time, I was going through an audition—the first ever open audition by national television in China—with another thousand college girls. The producer told us they were looking for some sweet, innocent and beautiful fresh face. So when it was my turn, I stood up and said, "Why [do] women's personalities on television always have to be beautiful, sweet, innocent and, you know, supportive? Why can't they have their own ideas and their own voice?" I thought I kind of offended them. But actually, they were impressed by my words. And so I was in the second round of competition, and then the third and the fourth. After seven rounds of competition, I was the last one to survive it. So I was on a national television prime-time show. And believe it or not, that was the first show on Chinese television that allowed its hosts to speak out of their own minds without reading an approved script. And my weekly audience at that time was between 200 and 300 million people.

Well, after a few years, I decided to go to the U.S. and Columbia University to pursue my postgraduate studies, and then started my own media company, which was unthoughtful of during the years that I started my career. So we do a lot of things. I've interviewed more than a thousand people in the past. And sometimes I have young people approaching me say, "Lan, you changed my life", and I feel proud of that. But then we are also so fortunate to witness the transformation of the whole country. I was in Beijing's bidding for the Olympic Games. I was representing the Shanghai Expo. I saw China embracing the world and vice versa. But then sometimes I'm thinking, what are today's young generation up to? How are they different, and what are the differences they are going to make to shape the future of China, or at large, the world?

So today *I want to talk about young people through the platform of social media.* First of all, who are they? [What] do they look like? Well, this is a girl called Guo Meimei—20 years old, beautiful. She showed off her expensive bags, clothes and car on her microblog, which is the Chinese version of Twitter. And she claimed to be the general manager of Red Cross at the Chamber of Commerce. She didn't realize that she stepped on a sensitive nerve and aroused national questioning, almost a turmoil, against the credibility of Red Cross. The controversy was so heated that the Red Cross had to open a press conference to clarify it, and the investigation is going on.

So far, as of today, we know that she herself made up that title—probably because she feels proud to be associated with charity. All those expensive items were given to her as gifts by her boyfriend, who used to be a board member in a subdivision of Red Cross at Chamber of Commerce. It's very complicated to explain. But anyway, the public still doesn't buy it. It is still boiling … And also it showed us the power and the impact of social media as microblog.

Microblog boomed in the year of 2010, with visitors doubled and time spent on it tripled. Sina.com, a major news portal, alone has more than 140 million micro-bloggers. On Tencent, 200 million. The most popular blogger—it's not me—it's a movie star, and she has more than 9.5 million followers, or fans. About 80 percent of those micro-bloggers are young people, under 30 years old …

So *through microblogging, we are able to understand Chinese youth even better.* So how are they different? First of all, most of them were born in the 80s and 90s … Most of them have fairly good education. The illiteracy rate in China among this generation is under one percent. In cities, 80 percent of kids go to college. But they are facing an aging China with a population above 65 years old coming up with seven-point-some percent this year, and about to be 15 percent by the year of 2030. And you know we have the tradition that younger generations support the elders financially, and taking care of them when they're sick. So it means young couples will have to support four parents who have a life expectancy of 73 years old.

So *making a living is not that easy for young people.* College graduates are not in short supply. In urban areas, college graduates find the starting salary is about 400 U.S. dollars a month, while the average rent is above $500. So what do they do? They have to share space—squeezed in very limited space to save money—and they call themselves "tribe of ants". And for those who are ready to get married and buy their apartments, they figured out they have to work for 30 to 40 years to afford their first apartments…

Among the 200 million migrant workers, 60 percent of them are young people. They find themselves sort of sandwiched between the urban areas and the rural areas. Most of them don't want to go back to the countryside, but they don't have the sense of belonging. They work for longer hours with less income, less social welfare. And they're more vulnerable to job losses, subject to inflation, tightening loans from banks, appreciation of the renminbi, or decline of demand from Europe or America for the products they produce. Last year, though, an appalling incident ... aroused a huge outcry from society about the isolation, both physical and mental, of these migrant workers.

For those who do return back to the countryside, they find themselves very welcome locally, because with the knowledge, skills and networks they have learned in the cities, with the assistance of the Internet, they're able to create more jobs, upgrade local agriculture and create new business in the less developed market. So in the past, in the coastal areas, they found themselves in a shortage of labor.

These diagrams show a more general social background. The first one is the Engels coefficient, which explains that the cost of daily necessities has dropped its percentage all through the past decade, in terms of family income, to about 37-some percent. But then in the last two years, it goes up again to 39 percent, indicating a rising living cost. The Gini coefficient has already passed the dangerous line of 0.4. Now it's 0.5 ... showing us the income inequality. And so you see this whole society getting frustrated about losing some of its mobility. And also, the bitterness and even resentment towards the rich and the powerful is quite widespread. So any accusations of corruption or backdoor dealings between authorities or business would arouse a social outcry or even unrest.

So through some of the hottest topics on microblogging, we can see what young people care most about ...

We heard about polluted air, polluted water ... And then lately, people are very concerned about cooking oil, because thousands of people have been found [refining] cooking oil from restaurant slop. So all these things have aroused a huge outcry from the Internet. And fortunately, we have seen the government responding more timely and also more frequently to the public concerns.

While young people seem to be very sure about their participation in public policy-making, but sometimes they're a little bit lost in terms of what they want for their personal life. China is soon to pass the U.S. as the number one market for luxury brands—that's not including the Chinese expenditures in Europe and elsewhere. But you know what, half of those consumers are earning a salary below 2,000 U.S. dollars. They're not rich at all.

They're taking those bags and clothes as a sense of identity and social status. And this is a girl explicitly saying on a TV dating show that she would rather cry in a BMW than smile on a bicycle. But of course, we do have young people who would still prefer to smile, whether in a BMW or [on] a bicycle.

So in the next picture, you see a very popular phenomenon called "naked" wedding, or "naked" marriage. It does not mean they will wear nothing in the wedding, but it shows that these young couples are ready to get married without a house, without a car, without a diamond ring and without a wedding banquet, to show their commitment to true love. And also, people are doing good through social media. And the first picture showed us that a truck caging 500 homeless and kidnapped dogs for food processing was spotted and stopped on the highway with the whole country watching through microblogging. People were donating money, dog food and offering volunteer work to stop that truck. And after hours of negotiation, 500 dogs were rescued. And here also people are helping to find missing children. A father posted his son's picture onto the Internet. After thousands of resends in relay, the child was found, and we witnessed the reunion of the family through microblogging.

So happiness is the most popular word we have heard through the past two years. Happiness is not only related to personal experiences and personal values, but also, it's about the environment. People are thinking about the following questions: Are we going to sacrifice our environment further to produce higher GDP? How are we going to perform our social and political reform to keep pace with economic growth, to keep sustainability and stability? And also, how capable is the system of self-correctness to keep more people content with all sorts of friction going on at the same time? I guess these are the questions people are going to answer. And *our younger generation are going to transform this country while at the same time being transformed themselves.*

Thank you very much.

Section I Pre-class Tasks

Directions: *Finish the following tasks before class.*

1. Watch and listen to the speech for the first time, and get the main idea of the speech.

2. Watch the speech for the second time and find the answers to the following questions.

(1) What is the close relationship between the young generation and the future of China?

(2) What are the characteristics of the Chinese youth, who were born in the 1980s and 1990s?

(3) There are at least four examples in the speech—three of them are positive and one is negative. What are they?

- When
- Who
- Where
- What
- The ending

(4) According to the speaker, what type of social environment does the young generation in China face?

(5) Do you agree/disagree with the speaker? Why or why not?

3. Design 5 open-ended questions to interview five other students at the English chat. Write down your questions and peer evaluation in Table 5.1.

Table 5.1 Questions and Peer Evaluation (5)

Questions	Peer Evaluation (appropriateness, grammatical accuracy)
1.	
2.	
3.	
4.	
5.	
Student evaluator signature	

Section II Language Focus

1. Words & Expressions

- **vendor** /ˈvendə(r)/ *n.* a person who sells things, for example, food or newspapers, usually outside on the street 小贩；摊贩
- **lyric** /ˈlɪrɪk/ *adj.* expressing a person's personal feelings and thoughts 抒情的
- **otherness** /ˈʌðənəs/ *n.* the quality of being different or strange 相异；奇特性；特别

- **interrogate** /ɪnˈterəgeɪt/ *v.* to ask sb. a lot of questions over a long period of time, especially in an aggressive way 审问；盘问
- **summon** /ˈsʌmən/ *v.* to order sb. to appear in court 传唤；传讯（出庭）
- **audition** /ɔːˈdɪʃn/ *n.* a short performance given by an actor, a singer, etc., so that sb. can decide whether they are suitable to act in a play, sing in a concert, etc.（拟进行表演者的）试演；试唱；试音
- **innocent** /ˈɪnəsnt/ *adj.* not guilty of a crime, etc.; not having done sth. wrong 无辜的；无罪的
- **postgraduate** /ˌpəʊstˈgrædʒuət/ *n.* a person who already holds a first degree and who is doing advanced study or research; a graduate student 研究生
- **microblog** /ˈmaɪkrəʊblɒg/ *n.* [Internet] a mini blog 微博
- **controversy** /ˈkɒntrəvɜːsi/ *n.* public discussion and argument about sth. that many people strongly disagree about, disapprove of, or are shocked by（公开的）争论；辩论；论战
- **subdivision** /ˌsʌbdɪˈvɪʒn/ *n.* the act of dividing a part of sth. into smaller parts 再分割；再分；细分
- **illiteracy** /ɪˈlɪtərəsi/ *n.* the state of not knowing how to read or write 文盲
- **skyrocket** /ˈskaɪrɒkɪt/ *v.* to rise quickly to a very high level（价格）飞涨，猛涨；（使）……猛然上涨
- **sandwich** /ˈsænwɪtʃ/ *v.* to fit sth./sb. into a very small space between two other things or people, or between two times 把……夹（或插）在……中间
- **isolation** /ˌaɪsəˈleɪʃn/ *n.* the act of separating sb./sth.; the state of being separate 隔离；隔离状态
- **coefficient** /ˌkəʊɪˈfɪʃnt/ *n.* a number which is placed before another quantity and which multiplies it 系数
- **inequality** /ˌɪnɪˈkwɒləti/ *n.* the unfair difference between groups of people in society, when some have more wealth, status or opportunities than others 不平等；不平衡；不平均
- **corruption** /kəˈrʌpʃn/ *n.* dishonest or illegal behavior, especially of people in authority 腐败；贪污；贿赂；受贿
- **expenditure** /ɪkˈspendɪtʃə/ *n.* the act of spending or using money; an amount of money spent 花费；消费；费用；开支
- **kidnap** /ˈkɪdnæp/ *v.* to take sb. away illegally and keep them as a prisoner, especially in order to get money or sth. else for returning them 劫持；绑架

- **negotiation** /nɪˌɡəʊʃiˈeɪʃn/ *n.* formal discussion between people who are trying to reach an agreement 谈判；磋商；协商
- **sacrifice** /ˈsækrɪfaɪs/ *v.* to give up sth. important or valuable to you in order to get or do sth. that seems more important 牺牲；舍弃
- **sustainability** /səˌsteɪnəˈbɪləti/ *n.* the property of being sustainable 耐久性
- **friction** /ˈfrɪkʃn/ *n.* the action of one object or surface moving against another 摩擦

2. Sentences for Further Understanding

    Directions：*Translate the following sentences from English into Chinese.*

- A vegetable vendor in Shanghai, who loves singing Western opera, but she didn't understand any English or French or Italian, so she managed to fill in the lyrics with vegetable names in Chinese.
- They were the least expected to be successful in the business called entertainment, yet their courage and talent brought them through.
- We are all different from different perspectives. But I think being different is good, because you present a different point of view. You may have the chance to make a difference.
- My generation has been very fortunate to witness and participate in the historic transformation of China that has made so many changes in the past 20, 30 years.
- The producer told us they were looking for some sweet, innocent and beautiful fresh face.
- The first show on Chinese television that allowed its hosts to speak out of their own minds without reading an approved script.
- But then we are also so fortunate to witness the transformation of the whole country.
- What are the differences they are going to make to shape the future of China, or at large, the world?
- So today I want to talk about young people through the platform of social media.
- The controversy was so heated that the Red Cross had to open a press conference to clarify it, and the investigation is going on.
- And also it showed us the power and the impact of social media as microblog.
- Microblog boomed in the year of 2010, with visitors doubled and time spent on it tripled.
- They find themselves sort of sandwiched between the urban areas and the rural areas. Most of them don't want to go back to the countryside, but they don't have the sense

of belonging.
- They're able to create more jobs, upgrade local agriculture and create new business in the less developed market.
- So the good news is that earlier this year, the state council passed a new regulation on house requisition and demolition and passed the right to order forced demolition from local governments to the court.
- While young people seem to be very sure about their participation in public policy-making, but sometimes they're a little bit lost in terms of what they want for their personal life.
- Happiness is not only related to personal experiences and personal values, but also, it's about the environment.

Section III Outline of the Speech

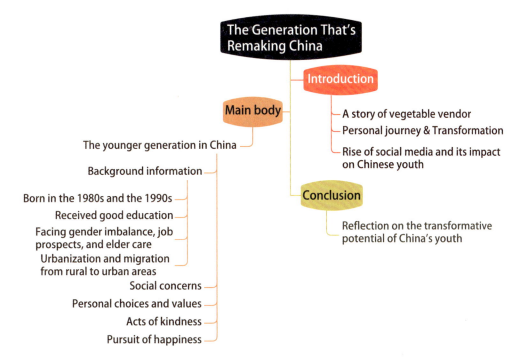

Section IV Public Speaking Skills

Good speeches need strong supporting materials to bolster the speaker's point of view. The three basic types of supporting materials are examples, statistics, and testimony.

In the course of a speech you may use brief examples—specific instances referred to in passing—and sometimes you may want to give several brief examples in a row to create a stronger impression. Extended examples are longer and more detailed. Hypothetical examples describe imaginary situations and can be quite effective for relating ideas to the audience.

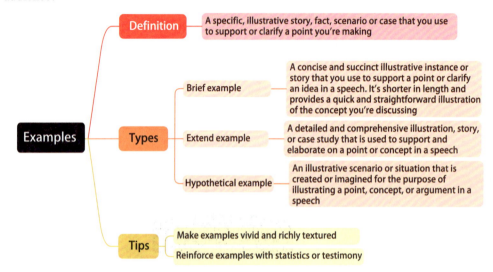

Section V English Chat Tasks

1. Q&A (5 questions): Work in groups to ask and answer questions prepared in the pre-class task.

2. A complete speech includes an introduction, main body and conclusion (Table 5.2). There are many techniques a speaker can use to create these parts of a speech. Discuss in groups what specific techniques the speaker uses in this speech and write down your answers.

Table 5.2 Sections and Techniques of the Speech(5)

Sections of a Speech	Techniques Used in a Speech	Techniques the Speaker Uses in the Speech
Introduction	1. Relate the topic to the audience 2. State the importance of your topic 3. Startle the audience 4. Arouse the curiosity of the audience 5. Question the audience 6. Begin with a quotation 7. Tell a story	

continued

Sections of a Speech	Techniques Used in a Speech	Techniques the Speaker Uses in the Speech
Main body	1. Evidence and examples 2. Explanation and analysis 3. Visual aids 4. Personal stories or anecdotes 5. Expert opinions or quotes 6. Transitions	
Conclusion	1. Signal the end of the speech 2. Summarize the speech 3. End with a quotation 4. Make a dramatic statement 5. Refer to the introduction	

Section VI EANLIC Party Tasks

1. Group Work

In groups, research an inspirational role model honored in annual Touching China Awards and deliver a speech about their life and achievements.

2. Prepared Speech

Three students will deliver prepared speeches each week. Score their work according to the feedback checklist below (Table 5.3).

Table 5.3 Checklist (5)

Checklist	Speech 1 1–5 From the least to the most	Speech 2 1–5 From the least to the most	Speech 3 1–5 From the least to the most
Is the speech well-prepared?	1 2 3 4 5	1 2 3 4 5	1 2 3 4 5
Was the speaker's voice loud enough?	1 2 3 4 5	1 2 3 4 5	1 2 3 4 5
Did the speaker look at the audience?	1 2 3 4 5	1 2 3 4 5	1 2 3 4 5
Did the speaker look confident?	1 2 3 4 5	1 2 3 4 5	1 2 3 4 5
Was there a clear and logical structure in the speech?	1 2 3 4 5	1 2 3 4 5	1 2 3 4 5
Were all the major claims supported by evidence?	1 2 3 4 5	1 2 3 4 5	1 2 3 4 5

	Speech 1	Speech 2	Speech 3
Checklist	1-5 From the least to the most	1-5 From the least to the most	1-5 From the least to the most
Have you found any mistakes in grammar/pronunciation?			
Do you have any suggestions for the speaker to improve next time?			

continued

3. Debate

Directions: *Work in groups to prepare a claim or counterclaim for the following idea beforehand, then participate in the debate at the EANLIC Party.*

Upon graduation, college students should prioritize returning to their hometown for employment over remaining in a metropolitan area.

4. Activities Focusing on Words and Expressions

Design an activity using words and expressions from the speech.

Section VII Assignment

Prepare a speech about "The Mission of the Young Generation".

Use examples to support your central ideas and make sure that your speech is well-articulated and captivating.

Unit 6   Why 30 Is Not the New 20

By Meg Jay

Learning Objectives

1. Achieve a thorough understanding of the speech contextually and linguistically.
2. Be able to express yourselves more freely on the topic of 20s.
3. Practice using stories when delivering a speech.
4. Learn about cherishing time and making a career plan.

Text

When I was in my 20s, I saw my very first psychotherapy client. I was a Ph.D. student in clinical psychology at Berkeley. She was a 26-year-old woman named Alex. Now Alex walked into her first session wearing jeans and a big slouchy top, and she dropped onto the couch in my office and kicked off her flats and told me she was there to talk about guy problems. Now when I heard this, I was so relieved. My classmate got an arsonist for her first client.

And I got a twentysomething who wanted to talk about boys. This I thought I could handle. But I didn't handle it. With the funny stories that Alex would bring to session, it was easy for me just to nod my head while we kicked the can down the road. "Thirty's the new 20," Alex would say, and as far as I could tell, she was right. Work happened later, marriage happened later, kids happened later, even death happened later. Twentysomethings like Alex and I had nothing but time.

But before long, my supervisor pushed me to push Alex about her love life. I pushed back. I said, "Sure, she's dating down, she's sleeping with a knucklehead, but it's not like she's going to marry the guy." And then my supervisor said, "Not yet, but she might marry the next one. Besides, the best time to work on Alex's marriage is before she has one."

That's what psychologists call an "Aha!" moment. That was the moment *I realized, 30 is not the new 20.* Yes, people settle down later than they used to, but that didn't make Alex's 20s a developmental downtime. That made Alex's 20s a developmental sweet spot, and we were sitting there, blowing it. That was when I realized that this sort of benign neglect was a real problem, and it had real consequences, not just for Alex and her love life but for the careers and the families and the futures of twentysomethings everywhere.

There are 50 million twentysomethings in the United States right now. We're talking about 15 percent of the population or 100 percent if you consider that no one's getting through adulthood without going through their 20s first.

Raise your hand if you're in your 20s. I really want to see some twentysomethings here. Oh, yay! You are all awesome. If you work with twentysomethings, you love a twentysomething, you're losing sleep over twentysomethings, I want to see—Okay. Awesome, twentysomethings really matter.

So, I specialize in twentysomethings because I believe that every single one of those 50 million twentysomethings deserves to know what psychologists, sociologists, neurologists and fertility specialists already know: *that claiming your 20s is one of the simplest, yet most transformative things you can do for work, for love, for your happiness, maybe even for the world.*

This is not my opinion. These are the facts. We know that *80 percent of life's most defining moments take place by age 35.* That means that 8 out of 10 of the decisions and experiences and "Aha!" moments that make your life what it is will have happened by your mid-30s. People who are over 40, don't panic. This crowd is going to be fine, I think. We know that *the first 10 years of a career has an exponential impact on how much money you're going to earn.* We know that more than half of Americans are married or are living with or dating their future partner by 30. We know that the brain caps off its second and last growth spurt in your 20s as it rewires itself for adulthood, which means that whatever it is you want to change about yourself, now is the time to change it. We know that personality changes more during your 20s than at any other time in life, and we know that female fertility peaks at age 28, and things get tricky after age 35. *So your 20s are the time to educate yourself about your body and your options.*

So when we think about child development, we all know that the first five years are a critical period for language and attachment in the brain. It's a time when your ordinary, day-to-day life has an inordinate impact on who you will become. But what we hear less about is that there's such a thing as adult development, and *our 20s are that critical period of adult development.*

But this isn't what twentysomethings are hearing. Newspapers talk about the changing timetable of adulthood. Researchers call the 20s an extended adolescence. Journalists coin silly nicknames for twentysomethings like "twixters" and "kidults". It's true!

As a culture, we have trivialized what is actually the defining decade of adulthood. Leonard Bernstein said that to achieve great things, you need a plan and not quite enough time. Isn't that true?

So what do you think happens when you pat a twentysomething on the head and you say, "You have 10 extra years to start your life"? Nothing happens. You have robbed that person of his urgency and ambition, and absolutely nothing happens.

And then every day, smart, interesting twentysomethings like you or like your sons and daughters come into my office and say things like this: "I know my boyfriend's no good for me, but this relationship doesn't count. I'm just killing time." Or they say, "Everybody says as long as I get started on a career by the time I'm 30, I'll be fine."

But then it starts to sound like this: "My 20s are almost over, and I have nothing to show for myself. I had a better resume the day after I graduated from college." And then it starts to sound like this: "Dating in my 20s was like musical chairs. Everybody was running around and having fun, but then sometime around 30 it was like the music turned off and everybody started sitting down. I didn't want to be the only one left standing up, so sometimes I think I married my husband because he was the closest chair to me at 30." Where are the twentysomethings here? Do not do that.

Okay, now that sounds a little flip, but make no mistake, the stakes are very high. When a lot has been pushed to your 30s, there is enormous thirtysomething pressure to jump—start a career, pick a city, partner up, and have two or three kids in a much shorter period of time. Many of these things are incompatible, and as research is just starting to show, simply harder and more stressful to do all at once in our 30s.

The post-millennial midlife crisis isn't buying a red sports car. It's realizing you can't have that career you now want. It's realizing you can't have that child you now want, or you can't give your child a sibling. Too many thirtysomethings and fortysomethings look at themselves, and at me, sitting across the room, and say about their 20s, "What was I doing? What was I thinking?" I want to change what twentysomethings are doing and thinking.

Here's a story about how that can go. It's a story about a woman named Emma. At 25, Emma came to my office because she was, in her words, having an identity crisis. She said she thought she might like to work in art or entertainment, but she hadn't decided yet, so she'd spent the last few years waiting tables instead. Because it was cheaper, she lived with a boyfriend who displayed his temper more than his ambition. And as hard as her 20s were, her early life had been even harder. She often cried in our sessions, but then would collect herself by saying, "You can't pick your family, but you can pick your friends."

Well one day, Emma comes in and she hangs her head in her lap, and she sobbed for most of the hour. She'd just bought a new address book, and she'd spent the morning filling in her many contacts, but then she'd been left staring at that empty blank that comes after the words "In case of emergency, please call …" She was nearly hysterical when she looked at me and said, "Who's going to be there for me if I get in a car wreck? Who's going to take care of me if I have cancer?"

Now at that moment, it took everything I had not to say, "I will." But what Emma needed wasn't some therapist who really, really cared. Emma needed a better life, and I knew this was her chance. I had learned too much since I first worked with Alex to just sit there while Emma's defining decade went parading by.

So over the next weeks and months, I told Emma three things that every twentysomething, male or female, deserves to hear.

First, I told Emma to *forget about having an identity crisis and get some identity capital.* By "get identity capital", I mean do something that adds value to who you are. Do something that's an investment in who you might want to be next. I didn't know the future of Emma's career, and no one knows the future of work, but I do know this: Identity capital begets identity capital. So now is the time for that cross-country job, that internship, that startup you want to try. I'm not discounting twentysomething exploration here, but I am discounting exploration that's not supposed to count, which, by the way, is not exploration. That's procrastination. I told Emma to explore work and make it count.

Second, I told Emma that *the urban tribe is overrated.* Best friends are great for giving rides to the airport, but twentysomethings who huddle together with like-minded peers limit who they know, what they know, how they think, how they speak, and where they work. That new piece of capital, that new person to date almost always comes from outside the inner circle. New things come from what are called our weak ties, our friends of friends of friends. So yes, half of twentysomethings are un- or under-employed.

But half aren't, and weak ties are how you get yourself into that group. Half of new jobs are never posted, so reaching out to your neighbor's boss is how you get that unposted job. It's not cheating. It's the science of how information spreads.

Last but not least, Emma believed that *you can't pick your family, but you can pick your friends.* Now this was true for her growing up, but as a twentysomething, soon Emma would pick her family when she partnered with someone and created a family of her own. I told Emma the time to start picking your family is now.

Now you may be thinking that 30 is actually a better time to settle down than 20, or even 25, and I agree with you. But grabbing whoever you're living with or sleeping with when everyone on Facebook starts walking down the aisle is not progress. *The best time to work on your marriage is before you have one, and that means being as intentional with love as you are with work. Picking your family is about consciously choosing who and what you want rather than just making it work or killing time with whoever happens to be choosing you.*

So what happened to Emma? Well, we went through that address book, and she found an old roommate's cousin who worked at an art museum in another state. That weak tie helped her get a job there. That job offer gave her the reason to leave that live-in boyfriend. Now, five years later, she's a special events planner for museums. She's married to a man she mindfully chose. She loves her new career, she loves her new family, and she sent me a card that said, "Now the emergency contact blanks don't seem big enough."

Now Emma's story made that sound easy, but that's what I love about working with twentysomethings. They are so easy to help. Twentysomethings are like airplanes just leaving LAX, bound for somewhere west. Right after takeoff, a slight change in course is the difference between landing in Alaska or Fiji. Likewise, at 21 or 25 or even 29, one good conversation, one good break, one good TED talk, can have an enormous effect across years and even generations to come.

So here's an idea worth spreading to every twentysomething you know. It's as simple as what I learned to say to Alex. It's what I now have the privilege of saying to twentysomethings like Emma every single day: *Thirty is not the new 20, so claim your adulthood, get some identity capital, use your weak ties, pick your family.* Don't be defined by what you didn't know or didn't do. *You're deciding your life right now.*

Thank you.

Section I Pre-class Tasks

Directions: *Finish the following tasks before class.*

1. Watch and listen to the speech for the first time, and get the main idea of the speech.

2. Watch the speech for the second time and find the answers to the following questions.

(1) What does the title "Why 30 is not the new 20" mean?

(2) Why is one's 20s the critical period of adult development? Find the proof from the speech.

(3) What are the consequences of delayed adulthood and the challenges faced by thirtysomethings?

(4) What are Meg Jay's suggestions for Emma? What is your understanding of them?

(5) How many stories are mentioned in the speech? What are they?

3. Design 5 open-ended questions to interview five other students at the English chat. Write down your questions and peer evaluation in Table 6.1.

Table 6.1 Questions and Peer Evaluation (6)

Questions	Peer Evaluation (appropriateness, grammatical accuracy)
1.	
2.	
3.	
4.	
5.	
Student evaluator signature	

Section II Language Focus

1. Words & Expressions

- **psychotherapy** /ˌsaɪkəʊˈθerəpi/ *n.* the treatment of mental illness by discussing sb.'s problems with them rather than by giving them drugs 心理治疗；精神治疗
- **relieved** /rɪˈliːvd/ *adj.* feeling happy because sth. unpleasant has stopped or has not

happened; showing this 感到宽慰的；放心的；宽心的

- **arsonist** /ˈɑːsənɪst/   *n.* a person who commits the crime of arson 纵火犯
- **supervisor** /ˈsuːpəvaɪzə(r)/   *n.* a person who supervises sb./sth. 监督人；指导者；主管人
- **knucklehead** /ˈnʌklhed/   *n.* a person who behaves in a stupid way 笨蛋；傻瓜
- **adulthood** /ˈædʌlthʊd/   *n.* the state of being an adult 成年
- **sociologist** /ˌsəʊsiˈɒlədʒɪst/   *n.* a person who studies sociology 社会学家
- **neurologist** /njʊəˈrɒlədʒɪst/   *n.* a doctor who studies and treats diseases of the nerves 神经病学家；神经科医生
- **fertility** /fəˈtɪləti/   *n.* the property of producing abundantly and sustaining vigorous and luxuriant growth 富饶；丰产；可繁殖性
- **transformative** /ˌtrænsˈfɔːmətɪv/   *adj.* causing a radical and typically positive change in outlook, character, form, or condition 有能力改革的
- **attachment** /əˈtætʃmənt/   *n.* if you have an attachment to sb. or sth., you are fond of them or loyal to them; an attachment is a device that can be fixed onto a machine in order to enable it to do different jobs 喜欢，爱慕，忠诚；（机器的）附件，附加装置
- **inordinate** /ɪnˈɔːdɪnət/   *adj.* far more than is usual or expected 过度的；过分的；超乎预料的
- **trivialize** /ˈtrɪviəlaɪz/   *v.* to make sth. seem less important, serious, difficult, etc. than it really is 使显得琐碎（或不重要、不难等）；轻视
- **incompatible** /ˌɪnkəmˈpætəbl/   *adj.* two actions, ideas, etc. that are incompatible are not acceptable or possible together because of basic differences （与某事物）不一致的；不相配的
- **post-millennial** /ˈpəʊstmɪˈleniəl/   *n.* of or relating to the period following the millennium 后千禧年
- **sibling** /ˈsɪblɪŋ/   *n.* a brother or sister 兄；弟；姐；妹
- **hysterical** /hɪˈsterɪkl/   *adj.* in a state of extreme excitement, and crying, laughing, etc. in an uncontrolled way 歇斯底里的；情绪狂暴不可抑止的
- **therapist** /ˈθerəpɪst/   *n.* a specialist who treats a particular type of illness or problem, or who uses a particular type of treatment （某治疗法的）治疗专家

2. Sentences for Further Understanding

Directions: *Translate the following sentences from English into Chinese.*

- Now Alex walked into her first session wearing jeans and a big slouchy top, and she dropped onto the couch in my office and kicked off her flats and told me she was there to talk about guy problems.
- With the funny stories that Alex would bring to session, it was easy for me just to nod my head while we kicked the can down the road.
- Work happened later, marriage happened later, kids happened later, even death happened later. Twentysomethings like Alex and I had nothing but time.
- That was when I realized that this sort of benign neglect was a real problem, and it had real consequences, not just for Alex and her love life but for the careers and the families and the futures of twentysomethings everywhere.
- Okay. Awesome, twentysomethings really matter.
- We know that 80 percent of life's most defining moments take place by age 35.
- This crowd is going to be fine, I think.
- We know that more than half of Americans are married or are living with or dating their future partner by 30.
- So when we think about child development, we all know that the first five years are a critical period for language and attachment in the brain.
- Journalists coin silly nicknames for twentysomethings like "twixters" and "kidults".
- As a culture, we have trivialized what is actually the defining decade of adulthood.
- Leonard Bernstein said that to achieve great things, you need a plan and not quite enough time.
- You have robbed that person of his urgency and ambition, and absolutely nothing happens.
- I know my boyfriend's no good for me, but this relationship doesn't count. I'm just killing time.
- My 20s are almost over, and I have nothing to show for myself. I had a better resume the day after I graduated from college.
- Where are the twentysomethings here? Do not do that.
- Many of these things are incompatible, and as research is just starting to show, simply harder and more stressful to do all at once in our 30s.
- The post-millennial midlife crisis isn't buying a red sports car.
- Right after takeoff, a slight change in course is the difference between landing in Alaska or Fiji. Likewise, at 21 or 25 or even 29, one good conversation, one good break, one good TED talk, can have an enormous effect across years and even

generations to come.
- Don't be defined by what you didn't know or didn't do. You're deciding your life right now.

Section III Outline of the Speech

Why 30 Is Not the New 20

- Introduction
  - A brief story
    - First client in psychotherapy
    - Realization: The 20s are a crucial developmental stage
- Main body
  - The importance of claiming your 20s
    - Statistics and research findings about significant life decisions and experiences occurring by age 35
    - Influence of the first 10 years of a career on earning potential
    - Biological and neurological factors shaping decisions and personality during the 20s
  - Addressing twentysomethings' concerns and challenges
    - Twentysomethings' narratives about relationships, careers, and identity crises
    - The pressure and consequences of delaying life decisions and actions
    - Guidance on how twentysomethings can navigate their 20s effectively
  - Emma's story: a case study
    - Introduction to Emma and her struggles in her 20s
    - Guidance provided for Emma
    - Emma's transformation and success as a result of claiming her adulthood
- Conclusion
  - Call to action for everyone to support and guide twentysomethings in claiming their adulthood
  - Urge twentysomethings to take control of their lives and make the most of their defining decade

Section IV Public Speaking Skills

Using stories in a speech is an effective way to engage your audience, make your message more memorable, and illustrate key points. Here's a step-by-step guide on how to use stories in your speech effectively.

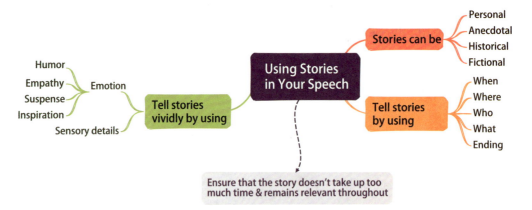

Section V English Chat Tasks

1. Q&A (5 questions): Work in groups to ask and answer questions prepared in the pre-class task.

2. A complete speech includes an introduction, main body and conclusion (Table 6.2). There are many techniques a speaker can use to create these parts of a speech. Discuss in groups what specific techniques the speaker uses in this speech and write down your answers.

Table 6.2 Sections and Techniques of the Speech (6)

Sections of a Speech	Techniques Used in a Speech	Techniques the Speaker Uses in the Speech
Introduction	1. Relate the topic to the audience 2. State the importance of your topic 3. Startle the audience 4. Arouse the curiosity of the audience 5. Question the audience 6. Begin with a quotation 7. Tell a story	

continued

Sections of a Speech	Techniques Used in a Speech	Techniques the Speaker Uses in the Speech
Main body	1. Evidence and examples 2. Explanation and analysis 3. Visual aids 4. Personal stories or anecdotes 5. Expert opinions or quotes 6. Transitions	
Conclusion	1. Signal the end of the speech 2. Summarize the speech 3. End with a quotation 4. Make a dramatic statement 5. Refer to the introduction	

Section VI EANLIC Party Tasks

1. Group Work

In groups, research an inspirational role model honored in annual Touching China Awards and deliver a speech about their life and achievements.

2. Prepared Speech

Three students will deliver prepared speeches each week. Score their work according to the feedback checklist below (Table 6.3).

Table 6.3 Checklist (6)

Checklist	Speech 1 1–5 From the least to the most	Speech 2 1–5 From the least to the most	Speech 3 1–5 From the least to the most
Is the speech well-prepared?	1 2 3 4 5	1 2 3 4 5	1 2 3 4 5
Was the speaker's voice loud enough?	1 2 3 4 5	1 2 3 4 5	1 2 3 4 5
Did the speaker look at the audience?	1 2 3 4 5	1 2 3 4 5	1 2 3 4 5
Did the speaker look confident?	1 2 3 4 5	1 2 3 4 5	1 2 3 4 5
Was there a clear and logical structure in the speech?	1 2 3 4 5	1 2 3 4 5	1 2 3 4 5
Were all the major claims supported by evidence?	1 2 3 4 5	1 2 3 4 5	1 2 3 4 5
Have you found any mistakes in grammar/pronunciation?			
Do you have any suggestions for the speaker to improve next time?			

3. Debate

Directions: *Work in groups to prepare a claim or counterclaim for the following idea beforehand, and then participate in the debate at the EANLIC Party.*

Some people believe that the 30 is the new 20, while others believe that 30 is not the new 20.

4. Activities Focusing on Words and Expressions

Design an activity using words and expressions from the speech.

Section VII Assignment

Share one challenge, dilemma, or hardship from your own life, what you have learned from the experience and how the experience will affect your future life.

Unit 7 How China Is Changing the Future of Shopping

By Angela Wang

Learning Objectives

1. Achieve a thorough understanding of the speech contextually and linguistically.
2. Learn to express yourselves more freely on the topic of shopping.
3. Be able to cite statistics in a speech to support the speaker's point.
4. Cultivate the sense of shopping rationally.

Text

This is my nephew, Yuan Yuan. He's five years old, super adorable. I asked him the other day, "What would you like for your birthday this year?" He said, "I want to have a one-way mirror Spider-Man mask." I had absolutely no idea what he was talking about, so I said, "Wow, that's really cool, but how are you going to get it?" He told me, without a blink of his eyes, "I'm going to tell my mom and make a wish before I go to bed. My mom will go to shake her mobile phone. The next morning, the delivery uncle will give it to me when I wake up." I was about to tease him, but suddenly I realized he was simply telling me the truth, the truth of what shopping looks like for this generation.

If you think of it, for a child like Yuan Yuan, shopping is a very different idea compared to what my generation had in mind. *Shopping is always done on mobile, and payment is all virtual.*

A huge shopping revolution is happening in China right now. Shopping behaviors, and also technology platforms, have evolved differently than elsewhere in the world. For instance, e-commerce in China is soaring. It's been growing at twice the speed of the United States and a lot of the growth is coming from mobile. Every month, 500 million consumers are buying on mobile phones, and to put that into context, that is a total population of the United States, UK and Germany combined. But it is not just about the scale of the e-commerce, it is the speed of adoption and the aggregation of the ecosystems. It took China less than five years to become a country of mobile commerce, and that is largely because of the two technology platforms, Alibaba and Tencent. They own 90 percent of the e-commerce—pretty much the whole market—85 percent of social media, 85 percent of Internet payment. And they also own large volumes of digital content, video, online movie, literature, travel information, gaming. When this huge base of mobile shoppers meets with aggregated ecosystems, chemical reactions happen. Today, China is like a huge laboratory generating all sorts of experiments. You should come to China, because here you will get a glimpse into the future.

One of the trends I have seen concerns the spontaneity of shopping. Five years ago, in a fashion study, we found that on average, a Chinese consumer would be buying five to eight pairs of shoes. This number tripled to reach about 25 pairs of shoes a year. Who would need so many pairs of shoes? So I asked them, "What are the reasons you buy?" They told me a list of inspirations: blogs, celebrity news, fashion information. But really, for many of them, there was no particular reason to buy. They were just browsing on their mobile site and then buying whatever they saw. We have observed the same level of spontaneity in everything, from grocery shopping to buying insurance products. But it is not very difficult to understand if you think about it. A lot of the Chinese consumers are still very new in their middle-class or upper-middle-class lifestyles, with a strong desire to buy everything new, new products, new services. And with this integrated ecosystem, it is so easy for them to buy, one clicks after another. *However, this new shopping behavior is creating a lot of challenges for those once-dominant businesses.* The owner of a fashion company told me that he's so frustrated because his customers keep complaining that his products are not new enough. Well, for a fashion company, really bad comment. And he already increased the number of products in each collection. It doesn't seem to work. So I told him there's something more important than that. You've got to give your consumer exactly what they want when they still want it. And he can learn something from the online apparel players in China. These companies, they collect real consumer feedback from mobile sites, from social media, and then their designers will translate this information into product ideas, and then send them to micro-studios for production. These micro-studios are really key in this overall ecosystem, because they take small orders, 30 garments at a time, and they can also make partially customized pieces. The fact that all these production designs are done locally, the whole process, from transporting to product on shelf or online sometimes takes only three to four days. That is super-fast, and that is highly responsive to what is in and hot on the market. And that is giving enormous headaches to traditional retailers who are only thinking about a few collections a year.

Then *there's a consumer's need for ultra convenience.* A couple of months ago, I was shopping with a friend in Tokyo. We were in the store, and there were three to four people standing in front of us at the checkout counter. Pretty normal, right? But both of us dropped our selection and walked away. This is how impatient we have become. Delivering ultra convenience is not just something nice to have. It is crucial to make sure your consumer actually buys. And *in China, we have learned that convenience is really the glue that will make online shopping a behavior and a habit that sticks.* It is sometimes more effective than a loyalty program alone. Take Hema for an example. It's a retail grocery concept developed by Alibaba. They deliver a full basket of products from 4,000 SKUs to your doorstep within 30 minutes. What is amazing is that they deliver literally everything: fruits, vegetables, of course. They also deliver live fish and also live Alaska king crab. Like my friend once told me, "It's really my dream coming true. Finally, I can impress my mother-in-law when she comes to visit me for dinner unexpectedly."

Well, companies like Amazon and FreshDirect are also experimenting in the same field. The fact that Hema is part of the Alibaba ecosystem makes it faster and also a bit easier to implement. For an online grocery player, it is very difficult, very costly, to deliver a full basket quickly, but for Hema, it's got a mobile app, it's got mobile payment, and also it's built 20 physical stores in high-density areas in Shanghai. These stores are built to ensure the freshness of the product—they actually have fish tanks in the store—and also to give locations that will enable high-speed delivery. I know the question you have on your mind. Are they making money? Yes, they are making money. They are breaking even, and what is also amazing is that the sales revenue per store is three to four times higher than in the traditional grocery store, and half of the revenue orders are coming from mobile. This is really proof that a consumer, if you give them ultra convenience that really works in grocery shopping, they're going to switch their shopping behaviors online, like, in no time.

So ultra convenience and spontaneity, that's not the full story. *The other trend I have seen in China is social shopping.* If you think of social shopping elsewhere in the world, it is a linear process. You pick up something on Facebook, watch it, and you switch to Amazon or brand.com to complete the shopping journey. Clean and simple. But in China it is a very different thing. On average, a consumer would spend one hour on their mobile phone shopping. That's three times higher than in the United States. Where does the stickiness come from? What are they actually doing on this tiny little screen? So let me take you on a mobile shopping journey that I usually would be experiencing.

11 pm, yes, that's usually when I shop. I was having a chat in a WeChat chatroom with my friends. One of them took out a pack of snack and posted the product link in that chatroom. I hate it, because usually I would just click that link and then land on the product page. Lots of information, very colorful, mind-blowing. Watched it and then a shop assistant came online and asked me, "How can I help you tonight?" Of course I bought that pack of snack. What is more beautiful is I know that the next day, around noontime, that pack of snack will be delivered to my office. I can eat it and share it with my colleagues and the cost of delivery, maximum one dollar.

Just when I was about to leave that shopping site, another screen popped up. This time it is the livestreaming of a grassroots celebrity teaching me how to wear a new color of lipstick. I watched for 30 seconds—very easy to understand—and also there is a shopping link right next to it, clicked it, bought it in a few seconds.

Back to the chatroom. The gossiping is still going on. Another friend of mine posted the QR code of another pack of snack. Clicked it, bought it. So the whole experience is like you're exploring in an amusement park. It is chaotic, it is fun and it's even a little bit addictive. This is what's happening when you have this integrated ecosystem. *Shopping is embedded in social, and social is evolving into a multidimensional experience.* The integration of ecosystems reaches a whole new level. So does its dominance in all aspects of our life.

And of course, *there are huge commercial opportunities behind it.* A Chinese snack company, Three Squirrels, built a half-a-billion-dollar business in just three years by investing in 300 to 500 shop assistants who are going to be online to provide services 24/7. In the social media environment, they are like your neighborhood friends. Even when you are not buying stuff, they will be happy to just tell you a few jokes and make you happy. *In this integrated ecosystem, social media can really redefine the relationship between brand, retailer and consumer.*

These are only fragments of the massive changes I have seen in China. In this huge laboratory, a lot of experiments are generated every single day. *The ecosystems are reforming, supply chain distribution, marketing, product innovation, everything. Consumers are getting the power to decide what they want to buy, when they want to buy it, and how they want to buy it, how they want to be social.* It is now back to business leaders of the world to really open their eyes, see what's happening in China, think about it and take actions. Thank you.

Massimo Portincaso: Angela, what you shared with us is truly impressive and almost incredible, but I think many in the audience had the same question that I had, which is: Is this kind of impulsive consumption both economically and environmentally sustainable over the longer term? And what is the total price to be paid for such an automatized and ultra convenient retail experience?

Angela Wang: Yeah. One thing we have to keep in mind is really, we are at the very beginning of a huge transformation. So with this trading up needs of the consumer, together with the evolution of the ecosystem, there are a lot of opportunities and also challenges. So I've seen some early signs that the ecosystems are shifting their focus to pay attention to solve these challenges. For example, paying more consideration to sustainability alongside just about speed, and also quality over quantity. But there are really no simple answers to these questions. That is exactly why I'm here to tell everyone that we need to watch it, study it, and play a part in this evolution.

Thank you very much.

Section I Pre-class Tasks

Directions: *Finish the following tasks before class.*

1. Watch and listen to the speech for the first time, and get the main idea of the speech.

2. Watch the speech for the second time and find the answers to the following questions.

(1) How do you describe new shopping habits in China?

(2) What are the challenges for those once-dominant businesses?

(3) What is impulsive consumption?

(4) What is social shopping?

(5) Normally there are three types of supporting materials in a speech: examples, statistics and testimony of experts or peers. What kind of supporting materials are used in this speech?

3. Design 5 open-ended questions to interview five other students at the English chat. Write down your questions and peer evaluation in Table 7.1.

Table 7.1 Questions and Peer Evaluation (7)

Questions	Peer Evaluation (appropriateness, grammatical accuracy)
1.	
2.	
3.	
4.	
5.	
Student evaluator signature	

Section II Language Focus

1. Words & Expressions

- **virtual** /ˈvɜːtʃuəl/ *adj.* made to appear to exist by the use of computer software, for example, on the Internet（通过计算机软件，如在互联网上）模拟的；虚拟的

- **evolve** /iˈvɒlv/ *v.* to develop gradually, especially from a simple to a more complicated form; to develop sth. in this way 发展；进化；（使）逐渐形成；逐渐演变

- **soar** /sɔː(r)/ *v.* if the value, amount or level of sth. soars, it rises very quickly 急升；猛增

- **aggregation** /ˌæɡrɪˈɡeɪʃn/ *n.* several things grouped together or considered as a whole 聚合；总量；集合体；聚合作用；凝聚；聚集作用

- **spontaneity** /ˌspɒntəˈneɪəti/ *n.* spontaneous, natural behavior 自然行为；自发动作

- **tripled** /ˈtrɪpld/ *adj.* consisting of three things or parts 三个的；三方的；三部分的

- **apparel** /əˈpærəl/ *n.* clothing, when it is being sold in shops/stores（尤指正式场合穿的）衣服；（商店出售的）服装

- **retailer** /ˈriːteɪlə(r)/ *n.* a person or business that sells goods to the public 零售商；零售店

- **doorstep** /ˈdɔːstep/ *n.* a step outside a door of a building, or the area that is very close to the door 门阶

- **chaotic** /keɪˈɒtɪk/ *adj.* in a state of complete confusion and lack of order 混乱的；杂乱的；紊乱的

- **embed** /ɪmˈbed/ *v.* if sth. such as an attitude or feeling is embedded in a society or

system, or in someone's personality, it becomes a permanent and noticeable feature of it 使（态度、感情等）植根于；使融入
- **multidimensional** /ˌmʌltɪdɪˈmenʃənl/ *adj.* having or involving or marked by several dimensions or aspects 多维的；多面的
- **fragment** /ˈfræɡmənt/ *n.* a small part of sth. that has broken off or comes from sth. larger 碎片；片断；小部分

2. Sentences for Further Understanding

Directions: *Translate the following sentences from English into Chinese.*

- Shopping behaviors, and also technology platforms, have evolved differently than elsewhere in the world.
- Every month, 500 million consumers are buying on mobile phones, and to put that into context, that is a total population of the United States, UK and Germany combined.
- Today, China is like a huge laboratory generating all sorts of experiments.
- We have observed the same level of spontaneity in everything, from grocery shopping to buying insurance products.
- These companies, they collect real consumer feedback from mobile sites, from social media, and then their designers will translate this information into product ideas, and then send them to micro-studios for production.
- In China, we have learned that convenience is really the glue that will make online shopping a behavior and a habit that sticks.
- It's really my dream coming true. Finally, I can impress my mother-in-law when she comes to visit me for dinner unexpectedly.
- This is really proof that a consumer, if you give them ultraconvenience that really works in grocery shopping, they're going to switch their shopping behaviors online, like, in no time.
- Shopping is embedded in social, and social is evolving into a multidimensional experience.
- Consumers are getting the power to decide what they want to buy, when they want to buy it, and how they want to buy it, how they want to be social.

Section III Outline of the Speech

Section IV Public Speaking Skills

Statistics in a speech refer to numerical data or information that is used to support, clarify, or illustrate a point or argument made during the presentation. Statistics can provide credibility, evidence, and a quantitative dimension to your speech, making your message more persuasive and informative. When using statistics in a speech, it's important to do so effectively and responsibly. Here are some tips for using statistics in a speech.

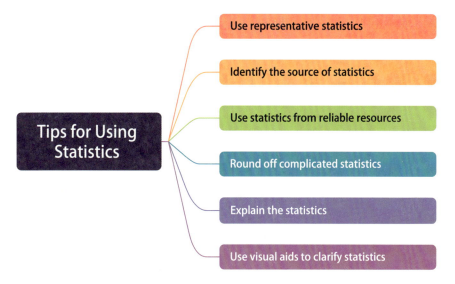

Explain statistics

Statistics don't speak for themselves. They need to be interpreted and related to your listeners. Here is an illustration of this concept on the topic of Chinese culture in the United States.

According to Jennifer Lee's The Fortune Cookie Chronicles, *there are some 43,000 Chinese restaurants in the U.S. That's more than all the McDonalds, Burger Kings, and KFCs combined.*

The speaker effectively provided context and relevance for the statistics to make them meaningful to the listeners.

Section V English Chat Tasks

1. Q&A (5 questions): Work in groups to ask and answer questions prepared in the pre-class task.

2. A complete speech includes an introduction, main body and conclusion (Table 7.2). There are many techniques a speaker can use to create these parts of a speech. Discuss in groups what specific techniques the speaker uses in this speech and write down your answers.

Table 7.2 Sections and Techniques of the Speech (7)

Sections of a Speech	Techniques Used in a Speech	Techniques the Speaker Uses in the Speech
Introduction	1. Relate the topic to the audience 2. State the importance of your topic 3. Startle the audience 4. Arouse the curiosity of the audience 5. Question the audience 6. Begin with a quotation 7. Tell a story	
Main body	1. Evidence and examples 2. Explanation and analysis 3. Visual aids 4. Personal stories or anecdotes 5. Expert opinions or quotes 6. Transitions	
Conclusion	1. Signal the end of the speech 2. Summarize the speech 3. End with a quotation 4. Make a dramatic statement 5. Refer to the introduction	

Section VI EANLIC Party Tasks

1. Group Work

In groups, research an inspirational role model honored in annual Touching China Awards and deliver a speech about their life and achievements.

2. Prepared Speech

Three students will deliver prepared speeches each week. Score their work according to the feedback checklist below (Table 7.3).

Table 7.3 Checklist (7)

Checklist	Speech 1 1–5 From the least to the most	Speech 2 1–5 From the least to the most	Speech 3 1–5 From the least to the most
Is the speech well-prepared?	1 2 3 4 5	1 2 3 4 5	1 2 3 4 5
Was the speaker's voice loud enough?	1 2 3 4 5	1 2 3 4 5	1 2 3 4 5
Did the speaker look at the audience?	1 2 3 4 5	1 2 3 4 5	1 2 3 4 5
Did the speaker look confident?	1 2 3 4 5	1 2 3 4 5	1 2 3 4 5

continued

Checklist	Speech 1 1–5 From the least to the most	Speech 2 1–5 From the least to the most	Speech 3 1–5 From the least to the most
Was there a clear and logical structure in the speech?	1 2 3 4 5	1 2 3 4 5	1 2 3 4 5
Were all the major claims supported by evidence?	1 2 3 4 5	1 2 3 4 5	1 2 3 4 5
Have you found any mistakes in grammar/pronunciation?			
Do you have any suggestions for the speaker to improve next time?			

3. Debate

Directions: *Work in groups to prepare a claim or counterclaim for the following idea beforehand, and then participate in the debate at the EANLIC Party.*

Whether the benefits of online shopping outweigh the traditional physical store shopping or not.

4. Activities Focusing on Words and Expressions

Design an activity by using new words and expressions from the speech.

Section VII Assignment

Tell a story about your impulsive consumption experience that addresses the following questions:

- What is the unforgettable impulsive consumption you experienced?
- Why did you buy the item at that time?
- What did you learn from that experience, or how would you handle it differently if faced with it again today?

Ensure that your story is well-expressed and engaging.

Unit 8 Every Kid Needs a Champion

By Rita Pierson

Learning Objectives

1. Achieve a thorough understanding of the speech contextually and linguistically.
2. Learn to express yourselves more freely on the topic of relationships between teachers and students.
3. Practice citing testimony in a speech to support the speaker's ideas.
4. Recognize the significant impact of good teacher-student relationships in education.

Text

I have spent my entire life either at the schoolhouse, on the way to the schoolhouse, or talking about what happens in the schoolhouse.

Both my parents were educators, my maternal grandparents were educators, and for the past 40 years, I've done the same thing. And so, needless to say, over those years I've had a chance to look at education reform from a lot of perspectives. Some of those reforms have been good. Some of them have been not so good. And we know why kids drop out. We know why kids don't learn. It's either poverty, low attendance, negative peer influences ... We know why. But *one of the things that we never discuss or we rarely discuss is the value and importance of human connection—relationships.*

James Comer says *that no significant learning can occur without a significant relationship.* George Washington Carver says *all learning is understanding relationships.* Everyone in this room has been affected by a teacher or an adult. For years, I have watched people teach. I have looked at the best and I've looked at some of the worst.

A colleague said to me one time, "They don't pay me to like the kids. They pay me to teach a lesson. The kids should learn it. I should teach it, and they should learn it. Case closed."

Well, I said to her, "You know, kids don't learn from people they don't like."

She said, "That's just a bunch of hooey."

And I said to her, "Well, your year is going to be long and arduous, dear."

Needless to say, it was. Some people think that you can either have it in you to build a relationship, or you don't. I think Stephen Covey had the right idea. He said you ought to just throw in a few simple things, like seeking first to understand, as opposed to being understood. Simple things, like apologizing. You ever thought about that? Tell a kid you're sorry, they're in shock.

I taught a lesson once on ratios. I'm not really good with math, but I was working on it.

And I got back and looked at that teacher edition. I'd taught the whole lesson wrong.

So I came back to class the next day and I said, "Look, guys, I need to apologize. I taught the whole lesson wrong. I'm so sorry."

They said, "That's okay, Ms. Pierson. You were so excited. We just let you go."

I have had classes that were so low, so academically deficient, that I cried. I wondered, "How am I going to take this group, in nine months, from where they are to where they need to be? And it was difficult, it was awfully hard. How do I raise the self-esteem of a child and his academic achievement at the same time?"

One year I came up with a bright idea. I told all my students, "You were chosen to be in my class because I am the best teacher and you are the best students. They put us all together so we could show everybody else how to do it."

One of the students said, "Really?"

I said, "Really. We have to show the other classes how to do it, so when we walk down the hall, people will notice us, so you can't make noise. You just have to strut."

And I gave them a saying to say: "I am somebody. I was somebody when I came. I'll be a better somebody when I leave. I am powerful, and I am strong. I deserve the education that I get here. I have things to do, people to impress, and places to go."

And they said, "Yeah!"

You say it long enough; it starts to be a part of you.

I gave a quiz, 20 questions. A student missed 18. I put a "+2" on his paper and a big smiley face.

He said, "Ms. Pierson, is this an F?"

He said, "Then why'd you put a smiley face?"

I said, "Because you're on a roll. You got two right. You didn't miss them all."

I said, "And when we review this, won't you do better?"

He said, "Yes, ma'am, I can do better."

You see, "-18" sucks all the life out of you. "+2" said, "I am not all bad."

For years, I watched my mother take the time at recess to review, go on home visits in the afternoon, buy combs and brushes and peanut butter and crackers to put in her desk drawer for kids that needed to eat, and a washcloth and some soap for the kids who didn't smell so good. See, it's hard to teach kids who stink.

And kids can be cruel. And so she kept those things in her desk, and years later, after she retired, I watched some of those same kids come through and say to her, "You know, Ms. Walker, you made a difference in my life. You made it work for me. You made me feel like I was somebody, when I knew, at the bottom, I wasn't. And I want you to just see what I've become."

And when my mama died two years ago at 92, there were so many former students at her funeral. It brought tears to my eyes, not because she was gone, but because *she left a legacy of relationships that could never disappear.*

Can we stand to have more relationships? Absolutely. Will you like all your children? Of course not.

And you know your toughest kids are never absent.

Never. You won't like them all, and the tough ones show up for a reason. It's the connection. It's the relationships. So teachers become great actors and great actresses, and we come to work when we don't feel like it, and we're listening to policy that doesn't make sense, and we teach anyway. We teach anyway, because that's what we do.

Teaching and learning should bring joy. How powerful would our world be if we had kids who were not afraid to take risks, who were not afraid to think, and who had a champion? *Every child deserves a champion, an adult who will never give up on them, who understands the power of connection, and insists that they become the best that they can possibly be.*

Is this job tough? You betcha. Oh God, you betcha. But it is not impossible. We can do this. We're educators. We're born to make a difference.

Thank you so much.

Section I Pre-class Tasks

Directions: *Finish the following tasks before class.*

1. Watch and listen to the speech for the first time, and get the main idea of the speech.

2. Watch the speech for the second time and find the answers to the following questions.

(1) What does the word "champion" mean?

(2) What is the key factor to motivate students to learn according to the speaker?

(3) How many stories did the speaker use to support her idea? And what are they?

(4) How many testimonies are used in the speech? And what are they?

(5) How to foster positive relationships with students?

3. Design 5 open-ended questions to interview five other students at the English chat. Write down your questions and peer evaluation in Table 8.1.

Table 8.1 Questions and Peer Evaluation (8)

Questions	Peer Evaluation (appropriateness, grammatical accuracy)
1.	
2.	
3.	
4.	
5.	
Student evaluator signature	

Section II Language Focus

1. Words & Expressions

- **maternal** /məˈtɜːnl/ *adj.* related through the mother's side of the family 母系的；母亲方面的

- **negative** /ˈneɡətɪv/ *adj.* considering only the bad side of sth./sb.; lacking enthusiasm or hope 消极的；负面的；缺乏热情的

- **peer** /pɪə(r)/ *n.* a person who is the same age or who has the same social status as you 同龄人；同辈；身份（或地位）相同的人；（英国）贵族成员

- **arduous** /ˈɑːdjuəs/ *adj.* involving a lot of effort and energy, especially over a period of time 艰苦的；艰难的

- **deficient** /dɪˈfɪʃnt/ *adj.* not having enough of sth. especially sth. that is essential 缺乏的；缺少的；不足的
- **self-esteem** /ˌself ɪˈstiːm/ *n.* a feeling of being happy with your own character and abilities 自尊（心）
- **academic achievement** 学术成就；学业成绩；学习成绩；学术成果
- **strut** /strʌt/ *v.* to walk proudly with your head up and chest out to show that you think you are important 高视阔步；趾高气扬地走；趾高气昂地走
- **deserve** /dɪˈzɜːv/ *v.* if sb./sth. deserves sth., it is right that they should have it, because of the way they have behaved or because of what they are 值得；应得；应受
- **cracker** /ˈkrækə(r)/ *n.* a thin dry biscuit that is often salty and usually eaten with cheese 薄脆饼干
- **stink** /stɪŋk/ *v.* to have a strong, unpleasant smell 有臭味；有难闻的气味
- **funeral** /ˈfjuːnərəl/ *n.* a ceremony, usually a religious one, for burying or cremating (= burning) a dead person 葬礼；丧礼；出殡
- **champion** /ˈtʃæmpiən/ *n.* a person, team, etc. that has won a competition, especially in a sport 冠军；优胜者；第一名

2. Sentences for Further Understanding

Directions：*Translate the following sentences from English into Chinese.*

- I have spent my entire life either at the schoolhouse, on the way to the schoolhouse, or talking about what happens in the schoolhouse.
- And so, needless to say, over those years I've had a chance to look at education reform from a lot of perspectives.
- We know why kids don't learn. It's either poverty, low attendance, negative peer influences ...
- But one of the things that we never discuss or we rarely discuss is the value and importance of human connection.
- You know that kids don't learn from people they don't like.
- Well, your year is going to be long and arduous, dear.
- He said you ought to just throw in a few simple things, like seeking first to understand, as opposed to being understood.
- I'm not really good with math, but I was working on it.
- I have had classes that were so low, so academically deficient, that I cried.

- How am I going to take this group, in nine months, from where they are to where they need to be?
- Teaching and learning should bring joy.
- You were chosen to be in my class because I am the best teacher and you are the best students. They put us all together so we could show everybody else how to do it.
- I am somebody. I was somebody when I came. I'll be a better somebody when I leave. I am powerful, and I am strong. I deserve the education that I get here. I have things to do, people to impress, and places to go.
- Because you're on a roll. You got two right. You didn't miss them all.
- Every child deserves a champion, an adult who will never give up on them, who understands the power of connection, and insists that they become the best that they can possibly be.

Section III Outline of the Speech

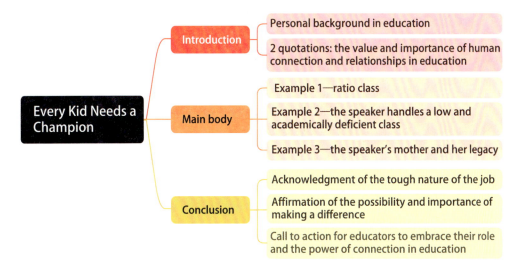

Section IV Public Speaking Skills

Testimony in a speech refers to the use of statements, quotes, or personal accounts from experts, witnesses, or individuals with relevant experience to support or illustrate a point, argument, or topic. Testimony can add credibility, real-life examples, and human perspectives to your speech. They can be used to persuade, inform, or engage the audience. Here's how to effectively use testimony in a speech.

Section V English Chat Tasks

1. Q&A (5 questions): Work in groups to ask and answer questions prepared in the pre-class task.

2. A complete speech includes an introduction, main body and conclusion (Table 8.2). There are many techniques a speaker can use to create these parts of a speech. Discuss in groups what specific techniques the speaker uses in this speech and write down your answers.

Table 8.2 Sections and Techniques of the Speech(8)

Sections of a Speech	Techniques Used in a Speech	Techniques the Speaker Uses in the Speech
Introduction	1. Relate the topic to the audience 2. State the importance of your topic 3. Startle the audience 4. Arouse the curiosity of the audience 5. Question the audience 6. Begin with a quotation 7. Tell a story	
Main body	1. Evidence and examples 2. Explanation and analysis 3. Visual aids 4. Personal stories or anecdotes 5. Expert opinions or quotes 6. Transitions	

continued

Sections of a Speech	Techniques Used in a Speech	Techniques the Speaker Uses in the Speech
Conclusion	1. Signal the end of the speech 2. Summarize the speech 3. End with a quotation 4. Make a dramatic statement 5. Refer to the introduction	

Section VI EANLIC Party Tasks

1. Group Work

In groups, research an inspirational role model honored in annual Touching China Awards and deliver a speech about their life and achievements.

2. Prepared Speech

Three students will deliver prepared speeches each week. Score their work according to the feedback checklist below (Table 8.3).

Table 8.3 Checklist (8)

Checklist	Speech 1 1–5 From the least to the most	Speech 2 1–5 From the least to the most	Speech 3 1–5 From the least to the most
Is the speech well-prepared?	1 2 3 4 5	1 2 3 4 5	1 2 3 4 5
Was the speaker's voice loud enough?	1 2 3 4 5	1 2 3 4 5	1 2 3 4 5
Did the speaker look at the audience?	1 2 3 4 5	1 2 3 4 5	1 2 3 4 5
Did the speaker look confident?	1 2 3 4 5	1 2 3 4 5	1 2 3 4 5
Was there a clear and logical structure in the speech?	1 2 3 4 5	1 2 3 4 5	1 2 3 4 5
Were all the major claims supported by evidence?	1 2 3 4 5	1 2 3 4 5	1 2 3 4 5
Have you found any mistakes in grammar/pronunciation?			
Do you have any suggestions for the speaker to improve next time?			

3. Debate

Directions: *Work in groups to prepare a claim or counterclaim for the following*

idea beforehand, *and then participate in the debate at the EANLIC Party.*

Some people believe that praising children can make them proud and arrogant, while others believe that praising children can help build their confidence.

4. Activities Focusing on Words and Expressions

Design an activity using words and expressions from the speech.

Section VII Assignment

Tell a story on "The Teacher Who Influenced Me the Most" that addresses the following questions:

- Who is your favorite teacher?
- Why do you like him or her most?
- In what ways has he or she influenced you?

Cite testimony in your speech and ensure that your story is well-expressed and engaging.

Unit 9 How Bees Can Keep the Peace Between Elephants and Humans

By Lucy King

Learning Objectives

1. Achieve a thorough understanding of the speech contextually and linguistically.
2. Improve ability to communicate with others about the relationship between animals and humans.
3. Develop a strong sense of speech organization.
4. Realize the importance of coexistence between humans and animals.

Text

Ever since I can remember, African elephants have filled me with a sense of complete awe. They are the largest land *mammal* alive today on planet Earth, weighing up to seven tons, standing three and a half meters tall at the shoulder. They can eat up to 400 kilos of food in a day, and they *disperse* vital plant seeds across thousands of kilometers during their 50-to-60-year lifespan.

Central to their compassionate and complex society are the matriarchs. These female, strong leaders nurture the young and navigate their way through the challenges of the African bush to find food, water and security. Their societies are so complex, we're yet to still fully tease apart how they communicate, how they verbalize to each other, and how their dialects work. And we don't really understand yet how they navigate the landscape, remembering the safest places to cross a river.

I'm pretty sure that like me, most of you in this room have a similar positive emotional response to these most magnificent of all animals. It's really hard not to have watched a documentary, learned about their intelligence or, if you've been lucky, to see them for yourselves on safari in the wild. But I wonder how many of you have been truly, utterly terrified by them.

I was lucky to be brought up in Southern Africa by two teacher parents who had long holidays but very short budgets. And so we used to take our old Ford Cortina Estate, and with my sister, we'd pile in the back, take our tents and go camping in the different game reserves in Southern Africa. It really was heaven for a young, budding zoologist like myself.

But I remember even at that young age that I found the tall electric fences blocking off the game parks quite divisive. Sure, they were keeping elephants out of the communities, but they also kept communities out of their wild spaces. It really was quite a challenge to me at that young age. It was only when I moved to Kenya at the age of 14, when I got to connect to the vast, wild open spaces of East Africa. And it is here now that I feel truly, instinctively, really at home.

I spent many, many happy years studying elephant behavior in a tent, in Samburu National Reserve, under the guidance of professor Fritz Vollrath and Iain Douglas-Hamilton, studying for my PhD and understanding the complexities of elephant societies. But now, in my role as head of the Human-Elephant Coexistence Program for Save the Elephants, we're seeing so much change happening so fast that it's urged a change in some of our research programs. No longer can we just sit and understand elephant societies or study just how to stop the ivory trade, which is horrific and still ongoing. *We're having to change our resources more and more to look at this rising problem of human-elephant conflict, as people and pachyderms compete for space and resources.*

It was only as recently as the 1970s that we used to have 1.2 million elephants roaming across Africa. Today, we're edging closer to only having 400,000 left. And at the same time period, the human population has quadrupled, and the land is being fragmented at such a pace that it's really hard to keep up with. Too often, these migrating elephants end up stuck inside communities, looking for food and water but ending up breaking open water tanks, breaking pipes and, of course, breaking into food stores for food. It's really a huge challenge. Can you imagine the terror of an elephant literally ripping the roof off your mud hut in the middle of the night and having to hold your children away as the trunk reaches in, looking for food in the pitch dark?

These elephants also trample and eat crops, and this is traditionally eroding away that tolerance that people used to have for elephants. And sadly, *we're losing these animals by the day and, in some countries, by the hour—to not only ivory poaching but this rapid rise in human-elephant conflict as they compete for space and resources.*

It's a massive challenge. I mean, how do you keep seven-ton pachyderms, that often come in groups of 10 or 12, out of these very small rural farms when you're dealing with people who are living on the very edge of poverty? They don't have big budgets. How do you resolve this issue?

Well, one issue is, you can just start to build electric fences, and this is happening across Africa. We're seeing this more and more. But they are dividing up areas and blocking corridors. And I'm telling you, these elephants don't think much of it either, particularly if they're blocking a really special water hole where they need water, or if there's a very attractive female on the other side. It doesn't take long to knock down one of these poles. And as soon as there's a gap in the fence, they go back, talk to their mates and suddenly they're all through, and now you have 12 elephants on the community side of the fence. And now you're really in trouble. People keep trying to come up with new designs for electric fences. Well, these elephants don't think much of those either.

So rather than having these hard-line, straight, electric, really divisive migratory-blocking fences, there must be other ways to look at this challenge. I'm much more interested in holistic and natural methods to keep elephants and people apart where necessary. Simply talking to people, talking to rural pastoralists in northern Kenya who have so much knowledge about the bush, we discovered this story that they had that elephants would not feed on trees that had wild beehives in them. Now this was an interesting story. As the elephants were foraging on the tree, they would break branches and perhaps break open a wild beehive. And those bees would fly out of their natural nests and sting the elephants.

Now if the elephants got stung, perhaps they would remember that this tree was dangerous and they wouldn't come back to the that same site. It seems impossible that they could be stung through their thick skin—elephant skin is around two centimeters thick. But it seems that they sting them around the watery areas, around the eyes, behind the ears, in the mouth, up the trunk. You can imagine they would remember that very quickly. And it's not really one sting that they're scared of. African bees have a phenomenal ability: when they sting in one site, they release a pheromone that triggers the rest of the bees to come and sting the same site. So it's not one bee sting that they're scared of—it's perhaps thousands of bee stings, coming to sting in the same area—that they're afraid of. And of course, a good matriarch would always keep her young away from such a threat. Young calves have much thinner skins, and it's potential that they could be stung through their thinner skins.

So for my PhD, I had this unusual challenge of trying to work out how African elephants and African bees would interact, when the theory was that they wouldn't interact at all. How was I going to study this? Well, what I did was I took the sound of disturbed African honey bees, and I played it back to elephants resting under trees through a wireless speaker system, so I could understand how they would react as if there were wild bees in the area. And it turns out that they react quite dramatically to the sound of African wild bees. Here we are, playing the bee sounds back to this amazing group of elephants. You can see the ears going up, going out. They're turning their heads from side to side. One elephant is flicking her trunk to try and smell. There's another elephant that kicks one of calves on the ground to tell it to get up as if there is a threat. And one elephant triggers a retreat, and soon the whole family of elephants are running after her across the savannah in a cloud of dust.

Now I've done this experiment many, many times, and the elephants almost always flee. Not only do they run away, but they dust themselves as they're running, as if to knock bees out of the air. And we placed infrasonic microphones around the elephants as we did these experiments. And it turns out they're communicating to each other in infrasonic rumbles to warn each other of the threat of bees and to stay away from the area.

So these behavioral discoveries really helped us understand how elephants would react should they hear or see bee sounds. This led me to invent a novel design for a beehive fence, which we are now building around small, one-to-two-acre farms on the most vulnerable frontline areas of Africa where humans and elephants are competing for space. These beehive fences are very, very simple. We use 12 beehives and 12 dummy hives to protect one acre of farmland. Now a dummy hive is simply a piece of plywood which we cut into squares, paint yellow and hang in between the hives. We're basically tricking the elephants into thinking there are more beehives than there really are. And of course, it literally halves the cost of the fence. So there's a hive and a dummy hive and a beehive and now dummy hive, every 10 meters around the outside boundary. They're held up by posts with a shade roof to protect the bees, and they're interconnected with a simple piece of plain wire, which goes all the way around, connecting the hives.

So if an elephant tries to enter the farm, he will avoid the beehive at all cost, but he might try and push through between the hive and the dummy hive, causing all the beehives to swing as the wire hits his chest. And as we know from our research work, this will cause the elephants to flee and run away—and hopefully remember not to come back to that risky area. The bees swarm out of the hive, and they really scare the elephants away.

These beehive fences we're studying using things like camera traps to help us understand how elephants are responding to them at night time, which is when most of the crop raiding occurs. And we found in our study farms that we're keeping up to 80 percent of elephants outside of the boundaries of these farms. And the bees and the beehive fences are also pollinating the fields. So we're having a great reduction both in elephant crop raids and a boost in yield through the pollination services that the bees are giving to the crops themselves.

The strength of the beehive fences is really important—the colonies have to be very strong. So we're trying to help farmers grow pollinator-friendly crops to boost their hives, boost the strength of their bees and, of course, produce the most amazing honey. This honey is so valuable as an extra livelihood income for the farmers. It's a healthy alternative to sugar, and in our community, it's a very valuable present to give a mother-in-law, which makes it almost priceless.

We now bottle up this honey, and we've called this wild beautiful honey Elephant-Friendly Honey. It is a fun name, but it also attracts attention to our project and helps people understand what we're trying to do to save elephants. We're working now with so many women in over 60 human-elephant conflict sites in 19 countries in Africa and Asia to build these beehive fences, working very, very closely with so many farmers but particularly now with women farmers, helping them to live better in harmony with elephants.

One of the things we're trying to do is develop a toolbox of options to live in better harmony with these massive pachyderms. One of those issues is to try and get farmers, and women in particular, to think different about what they're planting inside their farms as well. So we're looking at planting crops that elephants don't particularly want to eat, like chillies, ginger, Moringa, sunflowers. And of course, the bees and the beehive fences love these crops too, because they have beautiful flowers. One of these plants is a spiky plant called sisal—you may know this here as jute. And this amazing plant can be stripped down and turned into a weaving product.

We're working with these amazing women now who live daily with the challenges of elephants to use this plant to weave into baskets to provide an alternative income for them. We've just started construction only three weeks ago on a women's enterprise center where we're going to be working with these women not only as expert beekeepers but as amazing basket weavers; they're going to be processing chili oils, sunflower oils, making lip balms and honey, and we're somewhere on our way to helping these participating farmers live with better eco-generating projects that live and work better with living with elephants.

So whether it's matriarchs or mothers or researchers like myself, I do see more women coming to the forefront now to think differently and more boldly about the challenges that we face. *With more innovation, and perhaps with some more empathy towards each other, I do believe we can move from a state of conflict with elephants to true coexistence.*

Thank you.

Section I Pre-class Tasks

Directions: *Finish the following tasks before class.*

1. Watch and listen to the speech for the first time, and get the main idea of the speech.

2. Watch the speech for the second time and find the answers to the following questions.

(1) How could the elephants and humans live peacefully?

(2) What do you learn about elephants from the first paragraph?

(3) Why would the elephants not feed on trees that had wild beehives in them?

(4) How does the speaker organize the body of the speech?

(5) What are some of the benefits of using beehives to keep elephants away from crops?

3. Design 5 open-ended questions to interview five other students at the English chat. Write down your questions and peer evaluation in Table 9.1.

Table 9.1 Questions and Peer Evaluation (9)

Questions	Peer Evaluation (appropriateness, grammatical accuracy)
1.	
2.	
3.	
4.	
5.	
Student evaluator signature	

Section II Language Focus

1. Words & Expressions

- **disperse** /dɪˈspɜːs/ *v.* to spread or to make sth. spread over a wide area 散布；散发；传播

- **lifespan** /ˈlaɪfspæn/ *n.* the length of time that a member of a particular species can be expected to remain alive 寿命

- **compassionate** /kəmˈpæʃənət/ *adj.* feeling or showing sympathy for people who are suffering 有同情心的；表示怜悯的

- **matriarch** /ˈmeɪtriɑːk/ *n.* a woman who is the head of a family or social group 女家长；女族长

- **navigate** /ˈnævɪɡeɪt/ *v.* to find your position or the position of your ship, plane, car, etc. and the direction you need to go in, for example, by using a map 导航；确定（船、飞机、汽车等）的位置和方向

- **tease apart**   梳理

- **verbalize** /ˈvɜːbəlaɪz/ *v.* to express one's feelings or ideas in words 用言语（或文字）表达

- **magnificent** /mæɡˈnɪfɪsnt/ *adj.* extremely attractive and impressive; deserving praise 壮丽的；宏伟的；值得赞扬的

- **safari** /səˈfɑːri/ *n.* a trip to see or hunt wild animals, especially in east or southern Africa（尤指在非洲东部或南部的）观赏（或捕猎）野兽的旅行；游猎

- **utterly** /ˈʌtəli/ *adv.* completely, often used for emphasizing how bad someone or something is 完全地；绝对地

- **budding** /ˈbʌdɪŋ/ *adj.* beginning to develop or become successful 开始发展的；崭露头角的

- **divisive** /dɪˈvaɪsɪv/ *adj.* causing people to be split into groups that disagree with or oppose each other 造成不和的；引起分歧的；制造分裂的

- **instinctively** /ɪnˈstɪŋktɪvli/ *adv.* as a matter of instinct 本能地

- **horrific** /həˈrɪfɪk/ *adj.* extremely bad and shocking or frightening 极坏的；令人震惊的；令人惊恐的

- **pachyderm** /ˈpækidɜːm/ *n.* a large animal with thick skin, for example, an elephant or a rhinoceros 厚皮动物

- **quadruple** /kwɒˈdruːpl/ *v.* to become four times bigger; to make sth. four times

bigger （使）变为四倍
- **pitch dark** 漆黑
- **poach** /pəʊtʃ/ *v.* to illegally hunt birds, animals or fish on sb. else's property or without permission（在他人地界）偷猎；偷捕
- **phenomenal** /fə'nɒmɪnl/ *adj.* very great or impressive 了不起的；非凡的
- **pheromone** /'ferəməʊn/ *n.* a substance produced by an animal as a chemical signal, often to attract another animal of the same species 费洛蒙；外激素；信息素
- **rumble** /'rʌmbl/ *n.* a long deep sound or series of sounds 持续而低沉的声音；隆隆声
- **alternative** /ɔːl'tɜːnətɪv/ *n.* a thing that you can choose to do or have out of two or more possibilities 替换物
- **strip down** 拆开；剥开
- **empathy** /'empəθi/ *n.* the ability to understand another person's feelings, experience, etc. 同感；共鸣；同情

2. Sentences for Further Understanding

Directions: *Translate the following sentences from English into Chinese.*

- These female, strong leaders nurture the young and navigate their way through the challenges of the African bush to find food, water and security.
- Their societies are so complex, we're yet to still fully how they communicate, how they verbalize to each other, how their dialects work.
- It's really hard not to have watched a documentary, learned about their intelligence or, if you've been lucky, to see them for yourselves on safari in the wild.
- Sure, they were keeping elephants out of the communities, but they also kept communities out of their wild spaces.
- It was only when I moved to Kenya at the age of 14, when I got to connect to the vast, wild open spaces of East Africa. And it is here now that I feel truly, instinctively, really at home.
- No longer can we just sit and understand elephant societies or study just how to stop the ivory trade, which is horrific and still ongoing.
- And sadly, we're losing these animals by the day and, in some countries, by the hour—to not only ivory poaching but this rapid rise in human-elephant conflict as they compete for space and resources.
- People keep trying to come up with new designs for electric fences. Well, these elephants don't think much of those either.

- You can see the ears going up, going out. They're turning their heads from side to side. One elephant is flicking her trunk to try and smell.
- And as we know from our research work, this will cause the elephants to flee and run away—and hopefully remember not to come back to that risky area. The bees swarm out of the hive, and they really scare the elephants away.
- So we're trying to help farmers grow pollinator-friendly crops to boost their hives, boost the strength of their bees and, of course, produce the most amazing honey.
- This honey is so valuable as an extra livelihood income for the farmers. It's a healthy alternative to sugar, and in our community, it's a very valuable present to give a mother-in-law, which makes it almost priceless.
- We now bottle up this honey, and we've called this wild beautiful honey Elephant-Friendly Honey. It is a fun name, but it also attracts attention to our project and helps people understand what we're trying to do to save elephants.
- We're working with these amazing women now who live daily with the challenges of elephants to use this plant to weave into baskets to provide an alternative income for them.
- With more innovation, and perhaps with some more empathy towards each other, I do believe we can move from a state of conflict with elephants to true coexistence.

Section III Outline of the Speech

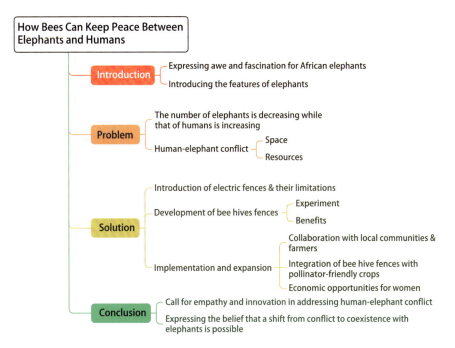

Section IV Public Speaking Skills

Audience have just a single opportunity to comprehend a speaker's ideas, and they have little patience for speakers who ramble aimlessly from one idea to another. A well-organized speech not only boosts your credibility but also facilitates the audience's comprehension of your message. Here are several common patterns for structuring the body of a speech (Table 9.2).

Table 9.2 Common Patterns for Structuring the Body of a Speech

Organizing the Body I	
Chronological order	The main points follow a time pattern. This is useful for explaining processes, historical events, or any subject that naturally follows a timeline.
Spatial order	The main points follow a directional pattern. This approach works well when describing places or giving directions.
Topical order	Arrange speech points based on specific topics or categories related to the main theme. This method is suitable for organizing information that doesn't follow a strict chronological sequence.
Problem-solution order	Identify a problem or issue and then propose solutions or actions. This is often used for persuasive or informative speeches that aim to address challenges and provide resolutions.
Problem-cause-solution order	First, identify a problem; then delve into its causes; and finally, offer solutions. This is a comprehensive way to address complex issues.
Cause and effect order	Explain the causes that lead to certain effects or consequences. This can help the audience understand the relationships between different factors.
Comparative order	Compare and contrast different aspects, ideas, or items. This structure helps the audience understand the similarities and differences between various elements.
Pro-con order	Present the pros and cons of a topic or issue. This is commonly used in persuasive speeches to help the audience make an informed decision.

Section V English Chat Tasks

1. Q&A (5 questions): Work in groups to ask and answer questions prepared in the pre-class task.

2. A complete speech includes an introduction, main body and conclusion (Table 9.2). There are many techniques a speaker can use to create these parts of a speech. Discuss in groups what specific techniques the speaker uses in this speech and write down your answers.

Table 9.2　Sections and Techniques of the Speech（9）

Sections of a Speech	Techniques Used in a Speech	Techniques the Speaker Uses in the Speech
Introduction	1. Relate the topic to the audience 2. State the importance of your topic 3. Startle the audience 4. Arouse the curiosity of the audience 5. Question the audience 6. Begin with a quotation 7. Tell a story	
Main body	1. Evidence and examples 2. Explanation and analysis 3. Visual aids 4. Personal stories or anecdotes 5. Expert opinions or quotes 6. Transitions	
Conclusion	1. Signal the end of the speech 2. Summarize the speech 3. End with a quotation 4. Make a dramatic statement 5. Refer to the introduction	

Section VI　EANLIC Party Tasks

1. Group Work

In groups, research an inspirational role model honored in annual Touching China Awards and deliver a speech about their life and achievements.

2. Prepared Speech

Three students will deliver prepared speeches each week. Score their work according to the feedback checklist below (Table 9.3).

Table 9.3　Checklist（9）

Checklist	Speech 1 1–5 From the least to the most	Speech 2 1–5 From the least to the most	Speech 3 1–5 From the least to the most
Is the speech well-prepared?	1　2　3　4　5	1　2　3　4　5	1　2　3　4　5
Was the speaker's voice loud enough?	1　2　3　4　5	1　2　3　4　5	1　2　3　4　5
Did the speaker look at the audience?	1　2　3　4　5	1　2　3　4　5	1　2　3　4　5
Did the speaker look confident?	1　2　3　4　5	1　2　3　4　5	1　2　3　4　5

continued

Checklist	Speech 1	Speech 2	Speech 3
	1–5 From the least to the most	1–5 From the least to the most	1–5 From the least to the most
Was there a clear and logical structure in the speech?	1 2 3 4 5	1 2 3 4 5	1 2 3 4 5
Were all the major claims supported by evidence?	1 2 3 4 5	1 2 3 4 5	1 2 3 4 5
Have you found any mistakes in grammar/pronunciation?			
Do you have any suggestions for the speaker to improve next time?			

3. Debate

Directions: *Work in groups to prepare a claim or counterclaim for the following idea beforehand, and then participate in the debate at the EANLIC Party.*

Some people think that humans and elephants can coexist, while others think that humans and elephants cannot coexist.

4. Activities Focusing on Words and Expressions

Design an activity using words and expressions from the speech.

Section VII Assignment

Tell a story about "Beautiful China".
- Use one of the organization patterns to arrange the body of your speech.
- Ensure that your story is well-expressed and engaging.

Unit 10 The Brain Changing Benefits of Exercise

By Wendy A. Suzuki

Learning Objectives

1. Achieve a thorough understanding of the speech contextually and linguistically.
2. Improve the ability to freely express personal views on the topic of exercise.
3. Use connections effectively when delivering a speech.
4. Recognize the crucial role exercise plays in maintaining healthy brain function and establish healthy exercise habits.

Text

What if I told you there was something that you can do right now that would have an immediate, positive benefit to your brain including your mood and your focus? And what if I told you that the same thing could actually last a long time and protect your brain from different conditions like depression, Alzheimer's disease or dementia. Would you do it? Yes!

I am talking about the powerful effects of physical activity. Simply moving your body, has immediate, long-lasting and protective benefits to your brain. And that can last for the rest of your life. So what I want to do today is to tell you a story about how I used my deep understanding of neuroscience, as a professor of neuroscience, to essentially do an experiment on myself in which I discovered the science underlying why exercise is the most transformative thing that you can do for your brain today. Now, as a neuroscientist, I know that our brains, that is the thing in our head right now, that is the most complex structure known to humankind. But it's one thing to talk about the brain, and it's another to see it.

So here is a real preserved human brain. And it's going to *illustrate* two key areas that we are going to talk about today. The first is the *prefrontal cortex*, right behind your forehead, critical for things like decision-making, focus, attention and your personality. The second key area is located in the temporal lobe, shown right here. You have two temporal lobes in your brain, the right and the left, and deep in the temporal lobe is a key structure critical for your ability to form and retain new long-term memories for facts and events. And that structure is called the *hippocampus*. So I've always been fascinated with the hippocampus. How could it be that an event that lasts just a moment, say, your first kiss, or the moment your first child was born, can form a memory that has changed your brain, that lasts an entire lifetime? That's what I want to understand. I wanted to start and record the activity of individual brain cells in the hippocampus as subjects were forming new memories, and essentially try and decode how those brief bursts of electrical activity, which is how neurons communicate with each other, how those brief bursts either allowed us to form a new memory, or did not.

But a few years ago, I did something very unusual in science. As a full professor of neural science, I decided to completely switch my research program. Because I encountered something that was so amazing, with the potential to change so many lives that I had to study it. I discovered and I experienced the brain-changing effects of exercise. And I did it in a completely inadvertent way. I was actually at the height of all the memory work that I was doing—data was pouring in. I was becoming known in my field for all of this memory work. And it should have been going great. It was scientifically. But when I stuck my head out of my lab door, I noticed something. I had no social life. I spent too much time listening to those brain cells in a dark room, by myself. I didn't move my body at all. I had gained 25 pounds. And actually, it took me many years to realize it, I was actually miserable. And I shouldn't be miserable. And I went on a river-rafting trip—by myself, because I had no social life. And I came back—thinking, "Oh, my God, I was the weakest person on that trip." And I came back with a mission. I said, "I'm never going to feel like the weakest person on a river-rafting trip again." And that's what made me go to the gym. And I focused my type-A personality on going to all the exercise classes at the gym. I tried everything. I went to kickboxing, dance, yoga, step class, and at first it was really hard. But what I noticed is that after every sweat-inducing workout that I tried, I had this great mood boost and this great energy boost. And that's what kept me going back to the gym. Well, I started feeling stronger. I started feeling better. I even lost that 25 pounds.

And now, fast-forward a year and a half into this regular exercise program and I noticed something that really made me sit up and take notice. I was sitting at my desk, writing a research grant, and a thought went through my mind that had never gone through my mind before. And that thought was, "Gee, grant-writing is going well today." And all the scientists—yeah, all the scientists always laugh when I say that, because grant-writing never goes well. It is so hard; you're always pulling your hair out, trying to come up with that million-dollar-winning idea. But I realized that the grant-writing was going well, because I was able to focus and maintain my attention for longer than I had before. And my long-term memory—what I was studying in my own lab—seemed to be better in me. And that's when I put it together.

Maybe all that exercise that I had included and added to my life was changing my brain. Maybe I did an experiment on myself without even knowing it. So as a curious neuroscientist, I went to the literature to see what I could find about what we knew about the effects of exercise on the brain. And what I found was an exciting and a growing literature that was essentially showing everything that I noticed in myself. Better mood, better energy, better memory, better attention. And *the more I learned, the more I realized how powerful exercise was*, which eventually led me to the big decision to completely shift my research focus. And so now, after several years of really focusing on this question, I've come to the following conclusion *that exercise is the most transformative thing that you can do for your brain today for the following three reasons.*

Number one: *it has immediate effects on your brain.* A single workout that you do will immediately increase levels of neurotransmitters like dopamine, serotonin and noradrenaline. That is going to increase your mood right after that workout, exactly what I was feeling. My lab showed, that a single workout can improve your ability to shift and focus attention, and that focus improvement will last for at least two hours. And finally, studies have shown that a single workout will improve your reaction times which basically means that you are going to be faster at catching that cup of Starbucks that falls off the counter, which is very, very important.

But these immediate effects are transient. They help you right after. What you have to do is do what I did, that is change your exercise regime, increase your cardiorespiratory function, to get the long-lasting effects. And these effects are long-lasting because exercise actually changes the brain's anatomy, physiology and function. Let's start with my favorite brain area, the hippocampus. The hippocampus—or exercise actually produces brand new brain cells, new brain cells in the hippocampus, that actually increase its volume, as well as improve your long-term memory, OK? And that including in you and me.

Number two: the most common finding in neuroscience studies, looking at effects of long-term exercise, is improved attention function dependent or your prefrontal cortex. *You not only get better focus and attention, but the volume of the hippocampus increases as well.* And finally, you not only get immediate effects of mood with exercise but those last for a long time. So you get long-lasting increases in those good mood neurotransmitters.

But really, *the most transformative thing that exercise will do is its protective effects on your brain.* Here you can think about the brain like a muscle. The more you're working out, the bigger and stronger your hippocampus and prefrontal cortex gets. Why is that important? Because the prefrontal cortex and the hippocampus are the two areas that are most susceptible to neurodegenerative diseases and normal cognitive decline in aging. *So with increased exercise over your lifetime, you're not going to cure dementia or Alzheimer's disease, but what you're going to do is you're going to create the strongest, biggest hippocampus and prefrontal cortex so it takes longer for these diseases to actually have an effect.* You can think of exercise, therefore, as a supercharged 401K for your brain, OK? And it's even better, because it's free.

So this is the point in the talk where everybody says, "That sounds so interesting, Wendy, but I really will only want to know one thing. And that is, just tell me the minimum amount of exercise I need to get all these changes."

And so I'm going to tell you the answer to that question. First, good news: you don't have to become a triathlete to get these effects. The rule of thumb is you want to get three to four times a week exercise minimum 30 minutes an exercise session, and you want to get aerobic exercise in. That is, get your heart rate up. And the good news is, you don't have to go to the gym to get a very expensive gym membership. Add an extra walk around the block in your power walk. You see stairs—take stairs. And power-vacuuming can be as good as the aerobics class that you were going to take at the gym.

So I've gone from memory pioneer to exercise explorer. From going into the innermost workings of the brain, to trying to understand how exercise can improve our brain function, and my goal in my lab right now is to go beyond that rule of thumb that I just gave you—three to four times a week, 30 minutes. I want to understand the optimum exercise prescription for you, at your age, at your fitness level, for your genetic background, to maximize the effects of exercise today and also to improve your brain and protect your brain the best for the rest of your life.

But it's one thing to talk about exercise, and it's another to do it. So I'm going to invoke my power as a certified exercise instructor, to ask you all to stand up.

We're going to do just one minute of exercise. It's call-and-response. Just do what I do, say what I say, and make sure you don't punch your neighbor, OK? Music!

Five, six, seven, eight, it's right, left, right, left. And I say, I am strong now. Let's hear you.

Audience: I am strong now.

Wendy Suzuki: Ladies, I am Wonder Woman-strong. Let's hear you!

Audience: I am Wonder Woman-strong.

Wendy Suzuki: New move—uppercut, right and left. I am inspired now. You say it!

Audience: I am inspired now.

Wendy Suzuki: Last move—pull it down, right and left, right and left. I say, I am on fire now! You say it.

Audience: I am on fire now.

Wendy Suzuki: And done! OK, good job!

Thank you. I want to leave you with one last thought. And that is, *bringing exercise in your life will not only give you a happier, more protective life today, but it will protect your brain from incurable diseases. And in this way it will change the trajectory of your life for the better.*

Thank you very much!

Section I Pre-class Tasks

Directions: *Finish the following tasks before class.*

1. Watch and listen to the speech for the first time, and get the main idea of the speech.

2. Watch the speech for the second time and find the answers to the following questions.

(1) According to the speaker, what benefits does exercise bring to your brain?

(2) What are the two key areas in human brain that the speaker mentioned and what are their functions?

(3) What benefits does the speaker get from exercise?

(4) According to the speaker, why is exercise considered the most transformative

thing you can do for your brain today?

(5) Identify connections in the speech and underline them.

3. Design 5 open-ended questions to interview five other students at the English chat. Write down your questions and peer evaluation in Table 10.1.

Table 10.1 Questions and Peer Evaluation (10)

Questions	Peer Evaluation (appropriateness, grammatical accuracy)
1.	
2.	
3.	
4.	
5.	
Student evaluator signature	

Section II Language Focus

1. Words & Expressions

- **depression** /dɪˈpreʃn/ *n.* a medical condition in which a person feels very sad and anxious and often has physical symptoms such as being unable to sleep, etc. 抑郁症；精神忧郁；沮丧；消沉

- **Alzheimer's disease** 阿尔茨海默病；老年痴呆症

- **dementia** /dɪˈmenʃə/ *n.* a serious mental disorder caused by brain disease or injury, which affects the ability to think, remember and behave normally 痴呆；精神错乱

- **neuroscience** /ˈnjʊərəʊsaɪəns/ *n.* the science that deals with the structure and function of the brain and the nervous system 神经科学

- **prefrontal** /priːˈfrʌntəl/ *adj.* anterior to a frontal structure 额叶前部的；前额的

- **cortex** /ˈkɔːteks/ *n.* the outer layer of an organ in the body, especially the brain 皮层；皮质；（尤指）大脑皮层

- **temporal lobe** 颞叶

- **retain** /rɪˈteɪn/ *v.* to keep sth.; to continue to have sth. 保持；持有；保留；继续拥有

- **hippocampus** /ˌhɪpəˈkæmpəs/ *n.* either of the two areas of the brain thought to be the centre of emotion and memory 海马（大脑中被认为是感情和记忆中心的部分）

- **fascinated** /ˈfæsɪneɪtɪd/ *adj.* if you are fascinated by sth., you find it very interesting and attractive, you tend to concentrate on it 极感兴趣的；入迷的
- **inadvertent** /ˌɪnədˈvɜːtənt/ *adj.* happening by chance or unexpectedly or unintentionally 无意的；并非故意的；因疏忽造成的
- **dopamine** /ˈdəʊpəmiːn/ *n.* a chemical produced by nerve cells which has an effect on other cells 多巴胺（神经细胞产生的一种作用于其他细胞的化学物质）
- **serotonin** /ˌserəˈtəʊnɪn/ *n.* a chemical produced naturally in your brain that affects the way you feel, for example, making you feel happier, calmer, or less hungry 血清素；五羟色胺（神经递质，亦影响情绪等）
- **noradrenaline** /ˌnɔːrəˈdrenəlin/ *n.* a catecholamine precursor of epinephrine that is secreted by the adrenal medulla and also released at synapses 去甲肾上腺素
- **transient** /ˈtrænziənt/ *adj.* continuing for only a short time 短暂的；转瞬即逝的
- **cardiorespiratory** /ˌkɑːdiəʊˈrespɪrətəri/ *adj.* of or pertaining to or affecting both the heart and the lungs and their functions 心肺的；心和肺的
- **anatomy** /əˈnætəmi/ *n.* the scientific study of the structure of human or animal bodies 解剖学
- **susceptible** /səˈseptəbl/ *adj.* very likely to be influenced, harmed or affected by sb./sth. 易受影响（或伤害等）的；敏感的；过敏的
- **supercharged** /ˈsuːpətʃɑːdʒd/ *adj.* powerful because it is supplied with air or fuel at a pressure that is higher than normal（用增压器）增压的，提高功率的
- **triathlete** /traɪˈæθlɪt/ *n.* someone who takes part in a triathlon 参加三项全能比赛的运动员
- **prescription** /prɪˈskrɪpʃn/ *n.* an official piece of paper on which a doctor writes the type of medicine you should have, and which enables you to get it from a chemist's shop/drugstore 处方；药方
- **trajectory** /trəˈdʒektəri/ *n.* the curved path of sth. that has been fired, hit or thrown into the air（射体在空中的）轨道；弹道；轨迹

2. Sentences for Further Understanding

Directions: *Translate the following sentences from English into Chinese.*

- Simply moving your body, has immediate, long-lasting and protective benefits for your brain.
- The first is the prefrontal cortex, right behind your forehead, critical for things like decision-making, focus, attention and your personality.

- So I've always been fascinated with the hippocampus.
- I wanted to start and record the activity of individual brain cells in the hippocampus as subjects were forming new memories.
- I discovered and I experienced the brain-changing effects of exercise.
- But what I noticed is that after every sweat-inducing workout that I tried, I had this great mood boost and this great energy boost.
- And now, fast-forward a year and a half into this regular exercise program and I noticed something that really made me sit up and take notice.
- You're always pulling your hair out, trying to come up with that million-dollar-winning idea.
- And the more I learned, the more I realized how powerful exercise was.
- Exercise is the most transformative thing that you can do for your brain today for the following three reasons.
- And finally, studies have shown that a single workout will improve your reaction times which basically means that you are going to be faster at catching that cup of Starbucks that falls off the counter, which is very, very important.
- The most common finding in neuroscience studies, looking at effects of long-term exercise, is improved attention function dependent or your prefrontal cortex.
- So I've gone from memory pioneer to exercise explorer.
- It's call-and-response. Just do what I do, say what I say, and make sure you don't punch your neighbor, OK?
- Bringing exercise in your life will not only give you a happier, more protective life today, but it will protect your brain from incurable diseases. And in this way it will change the trajectory of your life for the better.

Section III Outline of the Speech

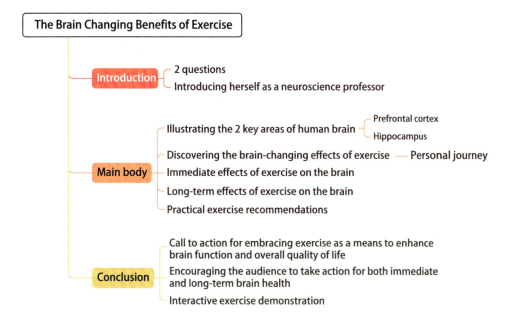

Section IV Public Speaking Skills

Connectives help tie a speech together. The four major types of speech connectives are transitions, internal previews, internal summaries, and signposts. Using them effectively will make your speeches more unified and coherent.

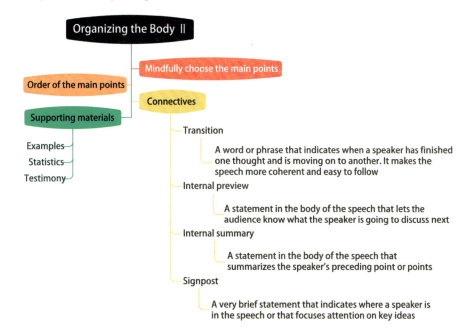

In the following examples, the connectives are underlined:

- <u>Now that</u> we have a clear understanding of the problem, <u>let me share</u> the solution with you. (*Transition*)

- In discussing how China has been stereotyped in the Western media, <u>we'll look first at the origins of the problem and second at its continuing impact today</u>. (*Internal preview*)

- <u>I've come to the following conclusion that exercise is the most transformative thing that you can do for your brain today for the following three reasons</u>. (*Internal summary*)

- <u>Number one:</u> it has immediate effects on your brain. <u>Number two:</u> the most common finding in neuroscience studies ... <u>And finally,</u> you not only get immediate effects of mood with exercise but those last for a long time. (*Signpost*)

Section V English Chat Tasks

1. Q&A (5 questions): Work in groups to ask and answer questions prepared in the pre-class task.

2. A complete speech includes an introduction, main body and conclusion (Table 10.2). There are many techniques a speaker can use to create these parts of a speech. Discuss in groups what specific techniques the speaker uses in this speech and write down your answers.

Table 10.2 Sections and Techniques of the Speech (10)

Sections of a Speech	Techniques Used in a Speech	Techniques the Speaker Uses in the Speech
Introduction	1. Relate the topic to the audience 2. State the importance of your topic 3. Startle the audience 4. Arouse the curiosity of the audience 5. Question the audience 6. Begin with a quotation 7. Tell a story	
Main body	1. Evidence and examples 2. Explanation and analysis 3. Visual aids 4. Personal stories or anecdotes 5. Expert opinions or quotes 6. Transitions	

continued

Sections of a Speech	Techniques Used in a Speech	Techniques the Speaker Uses in the Speech
Conclusion	1. Signal the end of the speech 2. Summarize the speech 3. End with a quotation 4. Make a dramatic statement 5. Refer to the introduction	

Section VI　EANLIC Party Tasks

1. Group Work

In groups, research an inspirational role model honored in annual Touching China Awards and deliver a speech about their life and achievements.

2. Prepared Speech

Three students will deliver prepared speeches each week. Score their work according to the feedback checklist below (Table 10.3).

Table 10.3　Checklist (10)

Checklist	Speech 1　1-5　From the least to the most	Speech 2　1-5　From the least to the most	Speech 3　1-5　From the least to the most
Is the speech well-prepared?	1　2　3　4　5	1　2　3　4　5	1　2　3　4　5
Was the speaker's voice loud enough?	1　2　3　4　5	1　2　3　4　5	1　2　3　4　5
Did the speaker look at the audience?	1　2　3　4　5	1　2　3　4　5	1　2　3　4　5
Did the speaker look confident?	1　2　3　4　5	1　2　3　4　5	1　2　3　4　5
Was there a clear and logical structure in the speech?	1　2　3　4　5	1　2　3　4　5	1　2　3　4　5
Were all the major claims supported by evidence?	1　2　3　4　5	1　2　3　4　5	1　2　3　4　5
Have you found any mistakes in grammar/pronunciation?			
Do you have any suggestions for the speaker to improve next time?			

3. Debate

Directions: *Work in groups to prepare a claim or counterclaim for the following*

idea beforehand, and then participate in the debate at the EANLIC Party.

Should daily exercise be a mandatory part of school curriculum to improve brain function and academic performance?

4. Activities Focusing on Words and Expressions

Design an activity using words and expressions from the speech.

Section VI Assignment

Prepare a speech about "My Favorite Sport". Your speech should address the following questions:

- What is your favorite sport? And why do you enjoy it?
- What benefits have you gained from the sport you like?

Please apply the connections in your speech. Make sure that your speech is unified and coherent.

Unit 11   What Makes a Good Life

By Robert Waldinger

Learning Objectives

1. Achieve a thorough understanding of the speech contextually and linguistically.
2. Learn to express yourselves more freely on the topic of a good life.
3. Practice utilizing effective speech ending techniques when delivering a speech.
4. Be aware of the importance of building good relationships.

Text

What keeps us healthy and happy as we go through life? If you were going to invest now in your future best self, where would you put your time and your energy? There was a recent survey of millennials asking them what their most important life goals were, and over 80 percent said that a major life goal for them was to get rich. And another 50 percent of those same young adults said that another major life goal was to become famous.

And we're constantly told to lean in to work, to push harder and achieve more. We're given the impression that these are the things that we need to go after in order to have a good life. Pictures of entire lives, of the choices that people make and how those choices work out for them, those pictures are almost impossible to get. Most of what we know about human life we know from asking people to remember the past, and as we know, hindsight is anything but 20/20. We forget vast amounts of what happens to us in life, and sometimes memory is downright creative.

But what if we could watch entire lives as they unfold through time? What if we could study people from the time that they were teenagers all the way into old age to see what really keeps people happy and healthy?

We did that. The Harvard Study of Adult Development may be the longest study of adult life that's ever been done. For 75 years, we've tracked the lives of 724 men, year after year, asking about their work, their home lives, their health, and of course asking all along the way without knowing how their life stories were going to turn out.

Studies like this are exceedingly rare. Almost all projects of this kind fall apart within a decade because too many people drop out of the study, or funding for the research dries up, or the researchers get distracted, or they die, and nobody moves the ball further down the field. But through a combination of luck and the persistence of several generations of researchers, this study has survived. About 60 of our original 724 men are still alive, still participating in the study, most of them in their 90s. And we are now beginning to study the more than 2,000 children of these men. And I'm the fourth director of the study.

Since 1938, we've tracked the lives of two groups of men. The first group started in the study when they were sophomores at Harvard College. They all finished college during World War II, and then most went off to serve in the war. And the second group that we've followed was a group of boys from Boston's poorest neighborhoods, boys who were chosen for the study specifically because they were from some of the most troubled and disadvantaged families in the Boston of the 1930s. Most lived in tenements, many without hot and cold running water.

When they entered the study, all of these teenagers were interviewed. They were given medical exams. We went to their homes and we interviewed their parents. And then these teenagers grew up into adults who entered all walks of life. They became factory workers and lawyers and bricklayers and doctors, one President of the United States. Some developed alcoholism. A few developed schizophrenia. Some climbed the social ladder from the bottom all the way to the very top, and some made that journey in the opposite direction.

The founders of this study would never in their wildest dreams have imagined that I would be standing here today, 75 years later, telling you that the study still continues. Every two years, our patient and dedicated research staff calls up our men and asks them if we can send them yet one more set of questions about their lives.

Many of the inner city Boston men ask us, "Why do you keep wanting to study me? My life just isn't that interesting." The Harvard men never ask that question.

To get the clearest picture of these lives, we don't just send them questionnaires. We interview them in their living rooms. We get their medical records from their doctors. We draw their blood. We scan their brains. We talk to their children. We videotape them talking with their wives about their deepest concerns. And when, about a decade ago, we finally asked the wives if they would join us as members of the study, and many of the women said, "You know, it's about time."

So what have we learned? What are the lessons that come from the tens of thousands of pages of information that we've generated on these lives? Well, the lessons aren't about wealth or fame or working harder and harder. *The clearest message that we get from this 75-year study is this: Good relationships keep us happier and healthier. Period.*

We've learned three big lessons about relationships. The first is that *social connections are really good for us, and that loneliness kills.* It turns out that people who are more socially connected to family, to friends, to community, are happier. They're physically healthier, and they live longer than people who are less well connected. And the experience of loneliness turns out to be toxic. People who are more isolated than they want to be from others find that they are less happy. Their health declines earlier in midlife. Their brain functioning declines sooner and they live shorter lives than people who are not lonely. And the sad fact is that at any given time, more than one in five Americans will report that they're lonely.

And we know that you can be lonely in a crowd and you can be lonely in a marriage, so the second big lesson that we learned is that it's not just the number of friends you have, and it's not whether or not you're in a committed relationship, but *it's the quality of your close relationships that matters.* It turns out that living in the midst of conflict is really bad for our health. High-conflict marriages, for example, without much affection, turn out to be very bad for our health, perhaps worse than getting divorced. And *living in the midst of good, warm relationships is protective.*

Once we had followed our men all the way into their 80s, we wanted to look back at them at midlife and to see if we could predict who was going to grow into a happy, healthy octogenarian and who wasn't. And when we gathered together everything we knew about them at age 50, it wasn't their middle age cholesterol levels that predicted how they were going to grow old. It was how satisfied they were in their relationships. The people who were the most satisfied in their relationships at age 50 were the healthiest at age 80. And good, close relationships seem to buffer us from some of the slings and arrows of getting old. Our most happily partnered men and women reported, in their 80s, that on the days when they had more physical pain, their mood stayed just as happy. But the people who were in unhappy relationships, on the days when they reported more physical pain, it was magnified by more emotional pain.

And the third big lesson that we learned about relationships and our health is that *good relationships don't just protect our bodies, they protect our brains.* It turns out that being in a securely attached relationship to another person in your 80s is protective, that the people who are in relationships where they really feel they can count on the other person in times of need, those people's memories stay sharper longer. And the people in relationships where they feel they really can't count on the other one, those are the people who experience earlier memory decline. And those good relationships don't have to be smooth all the time. Some of our octogenarian couples could bicker with each other day in and day out, but as long as they felt that they could really count on the other when the going got tough, those arguments didn't take a toll on their memories.

So this message, *that good, close relationships are good for our health and well-being, this is wisdom that's as old as the hills.* Why is this so hard to get and so easy to ignore? Well, we're human. What we'd really like is a quick fix, something we can get that'll make our lives good and keep them that way. Relationships are messy and they're complicated and the hard work of tending to family and friends, it's not sexy or glamorous. It's also lifelong. It never ends. The people in our 75-year study who were the happiest in retirement were the people who had actively worked to replace workmates with new playmates. Just like the millennials in that recent survey, many of our men when they were starting out as young adults really believed that fame and wealth and high achievement were what they needed to go after to have a good life. But over and over, over these 75 years, our study has shown that the people who fared the best were the people who leaned in to relationships, with family, with friends, with community.

So what about you? Let's say you're 25, or you're 40, or you're 60. What might leaning in to relationships even look like?

Well, the possibilities are practically endless. It might be something as simple as replacing screen time with people time or livening up a stale relationship by doing something new together, long walks or date nights, or reaching out to that family member who you haven't spoken to in years, because those all-too-common family feuds take a terrible toll on the people who hold the grudges.

I'd like to close with a quote from Mark Twain. More than a century ago, he was looking back on his life, and he wrote this: "There isn't time, so brief is life, for bickerings, apologies, heartburnings, callings to account. There is only time for loving, and but an instant, so to speak, for that."

The good life is built with good relationships.

Thank you.

Unit 11
What Makes a Good Life

Section I Pre-class Tasks

Directions: *Finish the following tasks before class.*

1. Watch and listen to the speech for the first time, and get the main idea of the speech.

2. Watch the speech for the second time and find the answers to the following questions.

（1）What is your understanding of "good life"?

（2）What is the goal of the Harvard Study of Adult Development? How is the study carried out? Who were the subjects in the study?

（3）What are the three important lessons to be learned about human relationships?

（4）What did you learn from the research team?

（5）How did the speaker end his speech?

3. Design 5 open-ended questions to interview five other students at the English chat. Write down your questions and peer evaluation in Table 11.1.

Table 11.1 Questions and Peer Evaluation（11）

Questions	Peer Evaluation (appropriateness, grammatical accuracy)
1.	
2.	
3.	
4.	
5.	
Student evaluator signature	

Section II Language Focus

1. Words & Expressions

- **millennial** /mɪˈleniəl/ *n.* people born in the millennium 千禧之子；千禧一代
- **hindsight** /ˈhaɪndsaɪt/ *n.* understanding the nature of an event after it has happened 后见之明
- **downright** /ˈdaʊnraɪt/ *adj.* characterized by plain blunt honesty（坏事或令人不快之事）彻头彻尾的；（人的举止或行为）直率的

- **unfold** /ʌnˈfəʊld/　*v.* to open, develop or come to a promising stage 打开，展开；呈现，逐渐明朗
- **exceedingly** /ɪkˈsiːdɪŋli/　*adv.* extremely 非常；极其
- **fall apart**　崩溃；土崩瓦解；破碎
- **distracted** /dɪˈstræktɪd/　*adj.* having the attention diverted especially because of anxiety 注意力分散的；心烦意乱的
- **sophomore** /ˈsɒfəmɔː/　*n.* a second-year undergraduate 大学二年级生
- **tenement** /ˈtenəmənt/　*n.* a rundown apartment house barely meeting minimal standards 公寓房间
- **bricklayer** /ˈbrɪkleɪə(r)/　*n.* a craftsman skilled in building with bricks 砖瓦工；砖匠
- **alcoholism** /ˈælkəhɒlɪzəm/　*n.* an intense persistent desire to drink alcoholic beverages to excess 酗酒；（内科）酒精中毒
- **schizophrenia** /ˌskɪtsəˈfriːniə/　*n.* any of several psychotic disorders characterized by distortions of reality and disturbances of thought and language and withdrawal from social contact（内科）精神分裂症
- **dedicated** /ˈdedɪkeɪtɪd/　*adj.* devoted to a cause or ideal or purpose 专用的；专注的；献身的
- **questionnaire** /ˌkwestʃəˈneə(r)/　*n.* a form containing a set of questions, submitted to people to gain statistical information 问卷；调查表
- **videotape** /ˈvɪdiəʊteɪp/　*v.* to record on videotape 将……录到录像带上
- **generate** /ˈdʒenəreɪt/　*v.* to bring into existence 产生；引发；生成
- **toxic** /ˈtɒksɪk/　*adj.* extremely harmful 极其有害的
- **decline** /dɪˈklaɪn/　*n.* a gradual falling off from a better state 下降；衰退
- **committed** /kəˈmɪtɪd/　*adj.* bound or obligated to a person or thing, as by pledge or assurance; devoted 尽心尽力的；忠诚的
- **glamorous** /ˈɡlæmərəs/　*adj.* having an air of allure, romance and excitement 迷人的；富有魅力的
- **octogenarian** /ˌɒktədʒəˈneəriən/　*n.* a person between 80 and 89 years old 八旬老人；80 至 89 岁的人
- **cholesterol** /kəˈlestərɒl/　*n.* a substance found in blood, fat and most tissues of the body 胆固醇
- **bicker** /ˈbɪkə(r)/　*v.* to argue or quarrel about unimportant things 斗嘴；争吵；发生口角

2. Sentences for Further Understanding

Directions: *Translate the following sentences from English into Chinese.*

- If you were going to invest now in your future best self, where would you put your time and your energy?
- We're given the impression that these are the things that we need to go after in order to have a good life.
- Pictures of entire lives, of the choices that people make and how those choices work out for them, those pictures are almost impossible to get.
- Most of what we know about human life we know from asking people to remember the past, and as we know, hindsight is anything but 20/20.
- We forget vast amounts of what happens to us in life, and sometimes memory is downright creative.
- But through a combination of luck and the persistence of several generations of researchers, this study has survived.
- It's not just the number of friends you have, and it's not whether or not you're in a committed relationship, but it's the quality of your close relationships that matters.
- What are the lessons that come from the tens of thousands of pages of information that we've generated on these lives?
- The first is that social connections are really good for us, and that loneliness kills.
- People who are more isolated than they want to be from others find that they are less happy, their health declines earlier in midlife, their brain functioning declines sooner and they live shorter lives than people who are not lonely.
- As long as they felt that they could really count on the other when the going got tough, those arguments didn't take a toll on their memories.
- So this message, that good, close relationships are good for our health and well-being, this is wisdom that's as old as the hills.
- What we'd really like is a quick fix, something we can get that'll make our lives good and keep them that way.
- There isn't time, so brief is life, for bickerings, apologies, heartburnings, callings to account.
- There is only time for loving, and but an instant, so to speak, for that.

Section III Outline of the Speech

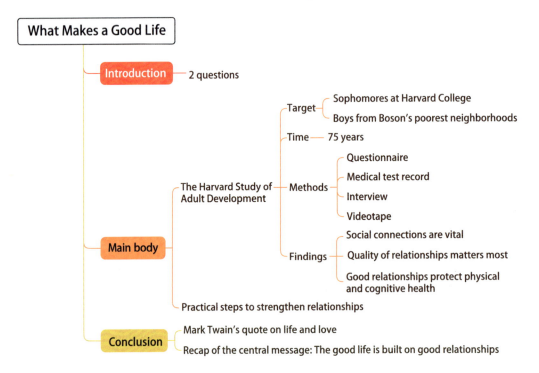

Section IV Public Speaking Skills

Ending a speech effectively is crucial to leave a lasting impression on your audience. Here are some tips on how to end a speech.

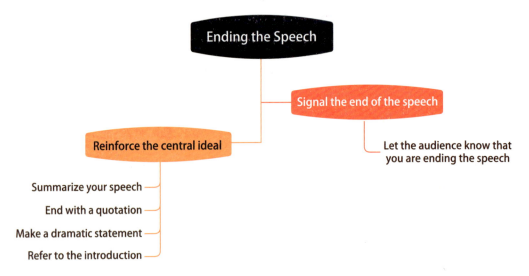

Section V English Chat Tasks

1. Q&A (5 questions): Work in groups to ask and answer questions prepared in the pre-class task.

2. A complete speech includes an introduction, main body and conclusion (Table 11.2). There are many techniques a speaker can use to create these parts of a speech. Discuss in groups what specific techniques the speaker uses in this speech and write down your answers.

Table 11.2 Sections and Techniques of the Speech(11)

Sections of a Speech	Techniques Used in a Speech	Techniques the Speaker Uses in the Speech
Introduction	1. Relate the topic to the audience 2. State the importance of your topic 3. Startle the audience 4. Arouse the curiosity of the audience 5. Question the audience 6. Begin with a quotation 7. Tell a story	
Main body	1. Evidence and examples 2. Explanation and analysis 3. Visual aids 4. Personal stories or anecdotes 5. Expert opinions or quotes 6. Transitions	
Conclusion	1. Signal the end of the speech 2. Summarize the speech 3. End with a quotation 4. Make a dramatic statement 5. Refer to the introduction	

Section VI EANLIC Party Tasks

1. Group Work

In groups, research an inspirational role model honored in annual Touching China Awards and deliver a speech about their life and achievements.

2. Prepared Speech

Three students will deliver prepared speeches each week. Score their work according to the feedback checklist below (Table 11.3).

Table 11.3　Checklist (11)

Checklist	Speech 1　1–5　From the least to the most	Speech 2　1–5　From the least to the most	Speech 3　1–5　From the least to the most
Is the speech well-prepared?	1　2　3　4　5	1　2　3　4　5	1　2　3　4　5
Was the speaker's voice loud enough?	1　2　3　4　5	1　2　3　4　5	1　2　3　4　5
Did the speaker look at the audience?	1　2　3　4　5	1　2　3　4　5	1　2　3　4　5
Did the speaker look confident?	1　2　3　4　5	1　2　3　4　5	1　2　3　4　5
Was there a clear and logical structure in the speech?	1　2　3　4　5	1　2　3　4　5	1　2　3　4　5
Were all the major claims supported by evidence?	1　2　3　4　5	1　2　3　4　5	1　2　3　4　5
Have you found any mistakes in grammar/pronunciation?			
Do you have any suggestions for the speaker to improve next time?			

3. Debate

Directions: *Work in groups to prepare a claim or counterclaim for the following idea beforehand, and then participate in the debate at the EANLIC Party.*

Some people believe that the key to happiness is achieving success and fame, while others believe that the key to happiness is having a good relationship with others.

4. Activities Focusing on Words and Expressions

Design an activity using words and expressions from the speech.

Section VII　Assignment

Prepare a speech about "How to Keep a Good Relationship with Others". Your speech should address the following questions and requirements:

- What is a good relationship?
- Why should we keep good relationships?
- How do you keep good relationships?

Ensure that your speech is well-articulated and ends with a vivid and forceful conclusion.

Unit 12　10 Ways to Have a Better Conversation

By Celeste Headlee

Learning Objectives

1. Achieve a thorough understanding of the speech contextually and linguistically.
2. Learn to express yourselves more freely on the topic of communication skills.
3. Be able to write the outline of a speech.
4. Be open to learning from others, fostering connection, and creating more enjoyable and valuable interactions.

Text

All right, I want to see a show of hands: how many of you have unfriended someone on Facebook because they said something offensive about politics or religion, childcare, food?

And how many of you know at least one person that you avoid because you just don't want to talk to them?

You know, it used to be that in order to have a polite conversation, we just had to follow the advice of Henry Higgins in "My Fair Lady": Stick to the weather and your health. But these days, with climate change and anti-vaxxing, those subjects—are not safe either. So this world that we live in, *this world in which every conversation has the potential to devolve into an argument*, where our politicians can't speak to one another and where even the most trivial of issues have someone fighting both passionately for it and against it, it's not normal. Pew Research did a study of 10,000 American adults, and they found that at this moment, we are more polarized, we are more divided, than we ever have been in history. *We're less likely to compromise, which means we're not listening to each other.* And we make decisions about where to live, who to marry and even who our friends are going to be, based on what we already believe. Again, that means we're not listening to each other. *A conversation requires a balance between talking and listening, and somewhere along the way, we lost that balance.*

Now, part of that is due to technology. The smartphones that you all either have in your hands or close enough that you could grab them really quickly. According to Pew Research, about a third of American teenagers send more than a hundred texts a day. And many of them, almost most of them, are more likely to text their friends than they are to talk to them face to face. There's this great piece in *The Atlantic*. It was written by a high school teacher named Paul Barnwell. And he gave his kids a communication project. He wanted to teach them how to speak on a specific subject without using notes. And he said this: "I came to realize ... "

"*I came to realize that conversational competence might be the single most overlooked skill we fail to teach.* Kids spend hours each day engaging with ideas and each other through screens, but rarely do they have an opportunity to hone their interpersonal communications skills. It might sound like a funny question, but we have to ask ourselves: Is there any 21st-century skill more important than being able to sustain coherent, confident conversation?"

Now, I make my living talking to people: Nobel Prize winners, truck drivers, billionaires, kindergarten teachers, heads of state, plumbers. I talk to people that I like. I talk to people that I don't like. I talk to some people that I disagree with deeply on a personal level. But I still have a great conversation with them. So I'd like to spend the next 10 minutes or so teaching you how to talk and how to listen.

Many of you have already heard a lot of advice on this, things like look the person in the eye, think of interesting topics to discuss in advance, look, nod and smile to show that you're paying attention, repeat back what you just heard or summarize it. So I want you to forget all of that. It is crap.

There is no reason to learn how to show you're paying attention if you are in fact paying attention.

Now, I actually use the exact same skills as a professional interviewer that I do in regular life. So, I'm going to teach you how to interview people, and that's actually going to help you learn *how to be better conversationalists*. Learn to have a conversation without wasting your time, without getting bored, and, without offending anybody.

We've all had really great conversations. We've had them before. We know what it's like. The kind of conversation where you walk away feeling engaged and inspired, or where you feel like you've made a real connection or you've been perfectly understood. There is no reason why most of your interactions can't be like that.

So I have *10 basic rules*. I'm going to walk you through all of them, but honestly, if you just choose one of them and master it, you'll already enjoy better conversations.

Number one: *Don't multitask.* And I don't mean just set down your cell phone or your tablet or your car keys or whatever is in your hand. I mean, be present. Be in that moment. Don't think about your argument you had with your boss. Don't think about what you're going to have for dinner. If you want to get out of the conversation, get out of the conversation, but don't be half in it and half out of it.

Number two: *Don't pontificate.* If you want to state your opinion without any opportunity for response or argument or pushback or growth, write a blog.

Now, there's a really good reason why I don't allow pundits on my show: Because they're really boring. If they're conservative, they're going to hate Obama and food stamps and abortion. If they're liberal, they're going to hate big banks and oil corporations and Dick Cheney. Totally predictable. And you don't want to be like that. You need to enter every conversation assuming that you have something to learn. The famed therapist M. Scott Peck said that true listening requires a setting aside of oneself. And sometimes that means setting aside your personal opinion. He said that sensing this acceptance, the speaker will become less and less vulnerable and more and more likely to open up the inner recesses of his or her mind to the listener. Again, assume that you have something to learn.

Bill Nye: "Everyone you will ever meet knows something that you don't." I put it this way: Everybody is an expert in something.

Number three: *Use open-ended questions.* In this case, take a cue from journalists. Start your questions with who, what, when, where, why or how. If you put in a complicated question, you're going to get a simple answer out. If I ask you, "Were you terrified?", you're going to respond to the most powerful word in that sentence, which is "terrified", and the answer is "Yes, I was" or "No, I wasn't." "Were you angry?" "Yes, I was very angry." Let them describe it. They're the ones that know. Try asking them things like, "What was that like?" "How did that feel?" Because then they might have to stop for a moment and think about it, and you're going to get a much more interesting response.

Number four: *Go with the flow.* That means thoughts will come into your mind and you need to let them go out of your mind. We've heard interviews often in which a guest is talking for several minutes and then the host comes back in and asks a question which seems like it comes out of nowhere, or it's already been answered. That means the host probably stopped listening two minutes ago because he thought of this really clever question, and he was just bound and determined to say that. And we do the exact same thing. We're sitting there having a conversation with someone, and then we remember that time that we met Hugh Jackman in a coffee shop.

And we stop listening. Stories and ideas are going to come to you. You need to let them come and let them go.

Number five: *If you don't know, say that you don't know.* Now, people on the radio, especially on NPR, are much more aware that they're going on the record, and so they're more careful about what they claim to be an expert in and what they claim to know for sure. Do that. Err on the side of caution. Talk should not be cheap.

Number six: *Don't equate your experience with theirs.* If they're talking about having lost a family member, don't start talking about the time you lost a family member. If they're talking about the trouble they're having at work, don't tell them about how much you hate your job. It's not the same. It is never the same. All experiences are individual. And, more importantly, it is not about you. You don't need to take that moment to prove how amazing you are or how much you've suffered. Somebody asked Stephen Hawking once what his IQ was, and he said, "I have no idea. People who brag about their IQs are losers."

Conversations are not a promotional opportunity.

Number seven: *Try not to repeat yourself.* It's condescending, and it's really boring, and we tend to do it a lot. Especially in work conversations or in conversations with our kids, we have a point to make, so we just keep rephrasing it over and over. Don't do that.

Number eight: *Stay out of the weeds.* Frankly, people don't care about the years, the names, the dates, all those details that you're struggling to come up with in your mind. They don't care. What they care about is you. They care about what you're like, what you have in common. So forget the details. Leave them out.

Number nine: This is not the last one, but it is the most important one. *Listen.* I cannot tell you how many really important people have said that listening is perhaps the most, the number one most important skill that you could develop. Buddha said, and I'm paraphrasing, "If your mouth is open, you're not learning." And Calvin Coolidge said, "No man ever listened his way out of a job."

Why do we not listen to each other? Number one, we'd rather talk. When I'm talking, I'm in control. I don't have to hear anything I'm not interested in. I'm the center of attention. I can bolster my own identity. But there's another reason: We get distracted. The average person talks at about 225 word per minute, but we can listen at up to 500 words per minute. So our minds are filling in those other 275 words. And look, I know, it takes effort and energy to actually pay attention to someone, but if you can't do that, you're not in a conversation. You're just two people shouting out barely related sentences in the same place.

You have to listen to one another. Stephen Covey said it very beautifully. He said, "Most of us don't listen with the intent to understand. We listen with the intent to reply."

One more rule, number 10, and it's this one: *Be brief.*

(A good conversation is like a miniskirt; short enough to retain interest, but long enough to cover the subject. — My Sister)

All of this boils down to the same basic concept, and it is this one: Be interested in other people.

You know, I grew up with a very famous grandfather, and there was kind of a ritual in my home. People would come over to talk to my grandparents, and after they would leave, my mother would come over to us, and she'd say, "Do you know who that was? She was the runner-up to Miss America. He was the mayor of Sacramento. She won a Pulitzer Prize. He's a Russian ballet dancer." And I kind of grew up assuming everyone has some hidden, amazing thing about them. And honestly, I think it's what makes me a better host. *I keep my mouth shut as often as I possibly can, I keep my mind open, and I'm always prepared to be amazed, and I'm never disappointed.*

You do the same thing. Go out, talk to people, listen to people, and, most importantly, be prepared to be amazed.

Section I Pre-class Tasks

Directions: *Finish the following tasks before class.*

1. Watch and listen to the speech for the first time, and get the main idea of the speech.

2. Watch the speech for the second time and find the answers to the following questions.

(1) What is a good and meaningful conversation?

（2）What are the challenges of modern conversations?

（3）Why do we not listen to each other?

（4）What are the ten basic rules to improve conversational skills?

（5）How do you handle the situation when you meet strangers?

3. Design 5 open-ended questions to interview five other students at the English chat. Write down your questions and peer evaluation in Table 12.1.

Table 12.1　Questions and Peer Evaluation (12)

Questions	Peer Evaluation (appropriateness, grammatical accuracy)
1.	
2.	
3.	
4.	
5.	
Student evaluator signature	

Section II Languages Focus

1. Words & Expressions

- **trivial** /ˈtrɪviəl/　*adj.* not important or serious; not worth considering 不重要的；琐碎的；微不足道的
- **passionately** /ˈpæʃənətli/　*adv.* with very strong feelings about sth. or a strong belief in sth. 热情地；狂热地
- **polarize** /ˈpəʊləraɪz/　*v.* to form two very different groups, opinions, or situations that are completely opposite to each other, or to cause this to happen 两极分化；给与……极性
- **smartphone** /ˈsmɑːtfəʊn/　*n.* a mobile phone that also works as a small computer, allowing you to store information and write letters and reports 智能手机
- **conversationalist** /ˌkɒnvəˈseɪʃnəlɪst/　*n.* talker, communicator, speaker 谈话者；健谈者
- **pontificate** /pɒnˈtɪfɪkeɪt/　*v.* to give your opinions in a way that shows you think you are definitely right, especially when this annoys other people 自以为是地谈论；目空一切地议论

- **pushback** /ˈpʊʃbæk/ *n.* negative reaction to a change or to sth. new that has been （对变革、计划等的）推拒；抵制；拒绝
- **pundit** /ˈpʌndɪt/ *n.* someone who is an expert in a subject, and is often asked to talk to the public about that subject 专家；评论员；权威人士；学者；博学者
- **conservative** /kənˈsɜːvətɪv/ *adj.* not willing to accept much change, especially in the traditional values of society 保守的；守旧的；因循守旧的；（式样等）保守的
- **assuming** /əˈsjuːmɪŋ/ *conj.* supposing, suppose, let's say, say, if 假如；假设……为真
- **equate** /iˈkweɪt/ *v.* to consider sth. to be the same as sth. else 同等看待；使等同
- **condescend** /ˌkɒndɪˈsend/ *v.* to behave in a way that shows that you think you are more important or more intelligent than other people 屈尊；俯就；（对某人）表现出优越感
- **rephrase** /ˌriːˈfreɪz/ *v.* to say or write the same thing using different words 改变说法；重新措辞；改变措辞；改述；重复信息
- **bolster** /ˈbəʊlstə(r)/ *v.* to make sth. stronger or more effective 加强；改善
- **ritual** /ˈrɪtʃuəl/ *n.* a formal ceremony; sth. that you do regularly and always in the same way 习惯；程序；仪规；礼节
- **Pulitzer Prize** 普利策奖（又称普利策新闻奖，是新闻领域的国际最高奖项）

2. Sentences for Further Understanding

Directions: *Translate the following sentences from English into Chinese.*

- So this world that we live in, this world in which every conversation has the potential to devolve into an argument, where our politicians can't speak to one another and where even the most trivial of issues have someone fighting both passionately for it and against it, it's not normal.
- We're less likely to compromise, which means we're not listening to each other.
- A conversation requires a balance between talking and listening, and somewhere along the way, we lost that balance.
- I came to realize that conversational competence might be the single most overlooked skill we fail to teach.
- If you want to get out of the conversation, get out of the conversation, but don't be half in it and half out of it.
- He said that sensing this acceptance, the speaker will become less and less vulnerable and more and more likely to open up the inner recesses of his or her mind to the

listener.

- Go with the flow.
- All experiences are individual.
- Stay out of the weeds.
- No man ever listened his way out of a job.

Section III Outline of the Speech

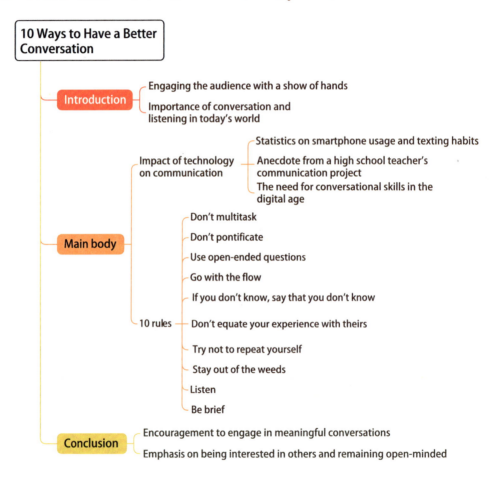

Section IV Public Speaking Skills

An outline is like a blueprint for your speech. It allows you to see the full scope and content of your speech at a glance. By outlining, you can judge whether each part of the speech is fully developed, whether you have adequate supporting materials for your main points, and whether the main points are properly balanced.

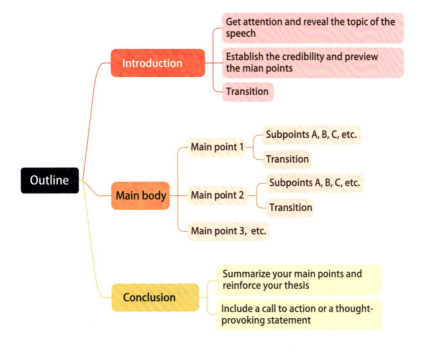

Section V English Chat Tasks

1. Q&A (5 questions): Work in groups to ask and answer questions prepared in the pre-class task.

2. A complete speech includes an introduction, main body and conclusion (Table 12.2). There are many techniques a speaker can use to create these parts of a speech. Discuss in groups what specific techniques the speaker uses in this speech and write down your answers.

Table 12.2 Sections and Techniques of the Speech (12)

Sections of a Speech	Techniques Used in a Speech	Techniques the Speaker Uses in the Speech
Introduction	1. Relate the topic to the audience 2. State the importance of your topic 3. Startle the audience 4. Arouse the curiosity of the audience 5. Question the audience 6. Begin with a quotation 7. Tell a story	

continued

Sections of a Speech	Techniques Used in a Speech	Techniques the Speaker Uses in the Speech
Main body	1. Evidence and examples 2. Explanation and analysis 3. Visual aids 4. Personal stories or anecdotes 5. Expert opinions or quotes 6. Transitions	
Conclusion	1. Signal the end of the speech 2. Summarize the speech 3. End with a quotation 4. Make a dramatic statement 5. Refer to the introduction	

Section VI EANLIC Party Tasks

1. Group Work

In groups, research an inspirational role model honored in annual Touching China Awards and deliver a speech about their life and achievements.

2. Prepared Speech

Three students will deliver prepared speeches each week. Score their work according to the feedback checklist below (Table 12.3).

Table 12.3 Checklist (12)

Checklist	Speech 1 1–5 From the least to the most	Speech 2 1–5 From the least to the most	Speech 3 1–5 From the least to the most
Is the speech well-prepared?	1 2 3 4 5	1 2 3 4 5	1 2 3 4 5
Was the speaker's voice loud enough?	1 2 3 4 5	1 2 3 4 5	1 2 3 4 5
Did the speaker look at the audience?	1 2 3 4 5	1 2 3 4 5	1 2 3 4 5
Did the speaker look confident?	1 2 3 4 5	1 2 3 4 5	1 2 3 4 5
Was there a clear and logical structure in the speech?	1 2 3 4 5	1 2 3 4 5	1 2 3 4 5
Were all the major claims supported by evidence?	1 2 3 4 5	1 2 3 4 5	1 2 3 4 5
Have you found any mistakes in grammar/pronunciation?			
Do you have any suggestions for the speaker to improve next time?			

3. Debate

Directions: *Work in groups to prepare a claim or counterclaim for the following idea beforehand, and then participate in the debate at the EANLIC Party.*

Is technology responsible for the younger generation's difficulty in initiating face-to-face conversations?

4. Activities Focusing on Words and Expressions

Design an activity using words and expressions from the speech.

Section VII Assignment

Prepare 5 questions to be used in a conversation with at least five students and teachers from the School of Foreign Languages at English chat, and then share answers and responses at the EANLIC Party.

Unit 13 Living Beyond Limits

By Amy Purdy

Learning Objectives

1. Achieve a thorough understanding of the speech contextually and linguistically.
2. Learn to express yourselves more freely on the topic of limits.
3. Use language accurately, clearly, appropriately and inclusively in a speech.
4. View life's challenges and limitations as opportunities for growth and innovation.

Text

If your life were a book and you were the author, how would you want your story to go? That's the question that changed my life forever. Growing up in the hot Las Vegas desert, all I wanted was to be free. I would daydream about traveling the world, living in a place where it snowed, and I would picture all of the stories that I would go on to tell.

At the age of 19, the day after I graduated from high school, I moved to a place where it snowed and I became a massage therapist. With this job all I needed were my hands and my massage table by my side and I could go anywhere. *For the first time in my life, I felt free, independent and completely in control of my life. That is, until my life took a detour.* I went home from work early one day with what I thought was the flu, and less than 24 hours later I was in the hospital on life support with less than a two percent chance of living. It wasn't until days later as I lay in a coma that the doctors diagnosed me with bacterial meningitis, a vaccine-preventable blood infection. Over the course of two and a half months I lost my spleen, my kidneys, the hearing in my left ear and both of my legs below the knee.

When my parents wheeled me out of the hospital, *I felt like I had been pieced back together like a patchwork doll.* I thought the worst was over until weeks later when I saw my new legs for the first time. The calves were bulky blocks of metal with pipes bolted together for the ankles and a yellow rubber foot with a raised rubber line from the toe to the ankle to look like a vein. I didn't know what to expect, but I wasn't expecting that.

With my mom by my side and tears streaming down our faces, I strapped on these chunky legs and I stood up. They were so painful and so confining that all I could think was, how am I ever going to travel the world in these things? How was I ever going to live the life full of adventure and stories, as I always wanted? And *how was I going to snowboard again?*

That day, I went home, I crawled into bed and this is what my life looked like for the next few months: me passed out, escaping from reality, with my legs resting by my side. I was absolutely physically and emotionally broken.

But I knew that in order to move forward, I had to let go of the old Amy and learn to embrace the new Amy. And that is when it dawned on me that I didn't have to be five-foot-five anymore. I could be as tall as I wanted! Or as short as I wanted, depending on who I was dating. And if I snowboarded again, my feet aren't going to get cold. And best of all, I thought, I can make my feet the size of all the shoes that are on the sales rack. And I did! So there were benefits here.

It was this moment that I asked myself that life-defining question: If my life were a book and I were the author, how would I want the story to go? And I began to daydream. I daydreamed like I did as a little girl and I imagined myself walking gracefully, helping other people through my journey and snowboarding again. And I didn't just see myself carving down a mountain of powder, I could actually feel it. I could feel the wind against my face and the beat of my racing heart as if it were happening at that very moment. *And that is when a new chapter in my life began.*

Four months later I was back up on a snowboard, although things didn't go quite as expected: My knees and my ankles wouldn't bend and at one point I traumatized all the skiers on the chair lift when I fell and my legs, still attached to my snowboard went flying down the mountain, and I was on top of the mountain still. I was so shocked, I was just as shocked as everybody else, and I was so discouraged, but I knew that if I could find the right pair of feet that I would be able to do this again. And this is when *I learned that our borders and our obstacles can only do two things: one, stop us in our tracks or two, force us to get creative.*

I did a year of research, but still couldn't figure out what kind of legs to use, and couldn't find any resources that could help me. So I decided to make a pair myself. My leg maker and I put random parts together and we made a pair of feet that I could snowboard in. As you can see, rusted bolts, rubber, wood and neon pink duct tape. And yes, I can change my toenail polish. It was these legs and the best 21st birthday gift I could ever receive—a new kidney from my dad—that allowed me to follow my dreams again. I started snowboarding, then I went back to work, and then I went back to school.

Then *in 2005 I cofounded a nonprofit organization for youth and young adults with physical disabilities so they could get involved with action sports.* From there, I had the opportunity to go to South Africa, where I helped to put shoes on thousands of children's feet so they could attend school.

And just this past February, *I won two back-to-back World Cup gold medals, which made me the highest ranked adaptive female snowboarder in the world.*

Eleven years ago, when I lost my legs, I had no idea what to expect. But if you ask me today, if I would ever want to change my situation, I would have to say no. Because my legs haven't disabled me, if anything they've enabled me. They've forced me to rely on my imagination and to believe in the possibilities, and that's why I believe that *our imaginations can be used as tools for breaking through borders, because in our minds, we can do anything and we can be anything.*

It's believing in those dreams and facing our fears head-on that allows us to live our lives beyond our limits. And although today is about innovation without borders, I have to say that in my life, innovation has only been possible because of my borders. *I've learned that borders are where the actual ends, but also where the imagination and the story begins.*

So the thought that I would like to challenge you with today is that maybe *instead of looking at our challenges and our limitations as something negative or bad, we can begin to look at them as blessings, magnificent gifts that can be used to ignite our imaginations and help us go further than we ever knew we could go.* It's not about breaking down borders. It's about pushing off of them and seeing what amazing places they might bring us. Thank you.

Section I Pre-class Tasks

Directions: *Finish the following tasks before class.*

1. Watch and listen to the speech for the first time, and get the main idea of the speech.

2. Watch the speech for the second time and find the answers to the following questions.

(1) What is your understanding of the title "Living Beyond Limits"?

(2) What was Amy Purdy's response to the loss of her spleen, kidneys, hearing in one ear and both of her legs?

(3) Can you imagine what kind of difficulties Amy would face after her loss?

(4) If you had the same illness as Amy, what would you do?

(5) What do you learn from the speaker?

3. Design 5 open-ended questions to interview five other students at the English chat. Write down your questions and peer evaluation in Table 13.1.

Table 13.1 Questions and Peer Evaluation (13)

Questions	Peer Evaluation (appropriateness, grammatical accuracy)
1.	
2.	
3.	
4.	
5.	
Student evaluator signature	

Section II Language Focus

1. Words & Expressions

- **daydream** /ˈdeɪdriːm/ v. to have absent-minded dreaming while awake; to have dreamlike musings or fantasies while awake 做白日梦；幻想；空想
- **picture** /ˈpɪktʃə(r)/ v. to imagine 想象；设想
- **massage therapist** 按摩师；按摩治疗师
- **detour** /ˈdiːtʊə(r)/ n. a longer route that you take in order to avoid a problem or to visit a place 绕行的路；迂回路；兜圈子
- **coma** /ˈkəʊmə/ n. a deep unconscious state, usually lasting a long time and caused by serious illness or injury 昏迷
- **diagnose** /ˈdaɪəgnəʊz/ v. to say exactly what an illness or the cause of a problem is 诊断（疾病）；判断（问题的原因）
- **meningitis** /ˌmenɪnˈdʒaɪtɪs/ n. a serious disease in which the tissues surrounding the brain and spinal cord become infected and swollen, causing severe headache, fever and sometimes death 脑膜炎；脑脊膜炎
- **vaccine** /ˈvæksiːn/ n. a substance that is put into the blood and that protects the body

from a disease 疫苗
- **infection** /ɪnˈfekʃn/ *n.* the act or process of causing or getting a disease 传染；感染
- **spleen** /spliːn/ *n.* a large dark-red oval organ on the left side of the body between the stomach and the diaphragm 脾；脾脏
- **patchwork** /ˈpætʃwɜːk/ *n.* a type of needlework in which small pieces of cloth of different colours or designs are sewn together（不同图案杂色布块的）拼缝物；拼布工艺
- **bulky** /ˈbʌlki/ *adj.* of large size for its weight 笨重的；庞大的
- **confine** /kənˈfaɪn/ *v.* to keep sb./sth. inside the limits of a particular activity, subject, area, etc. 限制；限定
- **embrace** /ɪmˈbreɪs/ *v.* to accept an idea, a proposal, a set of beliefs, etc. especially when it is done with enthusiasm; to put your arms around sb. as a sign of love or friendship 欣然接受，乐意采纳（思想、建议等）；拥抱
- **traumatize** /ˈtrɔːmətaɪz/ *v.* to shock and upset sb. very much, often making them unable to think or work normally 使受精神创伤
- **nonprofit** /ˌnɒnˈprɒfɪt/ *adj.* a non-profit organization is one which is not run with the aim of making a profit 非营利的
- **adaptive** /əˈdæptɪv/ *adj.* having the ability or tendency to adapt to different situations 适应的；有适应能力的

2. Sentences for Further Understanding

Directions: *Translate the following sentences from English into Chinese.*

- I would daydream about traveling the world, living in a place where it snowed, and I would picture all of the stories that I would go on to tell.
- For the first time in my life, I felt free, independent and completely in control of my life. That is, until my life took a detour.
- It wasn't until days later as I lay in a coma that the doctors diagnosed me with bacterial meningitis, a vaccine-preventable blood infection.
- I was absolutely physically and emotionally broken.
- But I knew that in order to move forward, I had to let go of the old Amy and learn to embrace the new Amy.
- It was this moment that I asked myself that life-defining question: If my life were a book and I were the author, how would I want the story to go? And I began to daydream.
- And that is when a new chapter in my life began.

- I cofounded a nonprofit organization for youth and young adults with physical disabilities so they could get involved with action sports.
- I won two back-to-back World Cup gold medals.
- Because my legs haven't disabled me, if anything they've enabled me. They've forced me to rely on my imagination and to believe in the possibilities, and that's why I believe that our imaginations can be used as tools for breaking through borders, because in our minds, we can do anything and we can be anything.
- It's believing in those dreams and facing our fears head-on that allows us to live our lives beyond our limits.
- And although today is about innovation without borders, I have to say that in my life, innovation has only been possible because of my borders. I've learned that borders are where the actual ends, but also where the imagination and the story begins.
- So the thought that I would like to challenge you with today is that maybe instead of looking at our challenges and our limitations as something negative or bad, we can begin to look at them as blessings, magnificent gifts that can be used to ignite our imaginations and help us go further than we ever knew we could go.

Section III Outline of the Speech

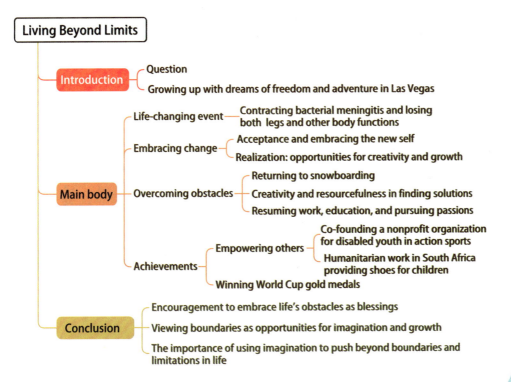

Section IV Public Speaking Skills

Good speakers respect language and how it works. It is essential for a speaker to employ language accurately, clearly, vividly, appropriately, and inclusively. Never use a word unless you are sure it is accurate. Using language clearly allows listeners to grasp your meaning immediately. Using language appropriately means adapting to the particular occasion, audience, and topic at hand. Using language inclusively is a vital component of fostering intercultural communicative competence. Here are some tips on how to use language in a speech (Table 13.2).

Table 13.2 Tips on How to Use Language in a Speech

Tips	How to Use Language in a Speech	
Accurately	Select the right words, arrange them in a grammatically correct manner, and express ideas in a way that reflects the intended message without ambiguity or confusion	
Clearly	Allow listeners to grasp your meaning immediately	
	Use familiar words	
	Choose concrete words	
	Eliminate clutter words	
Appropriately	Be appropriate to	the occasion
		the audience
		the topic
		the speaker
Inclusively	Avoid the generic "he"	
	Drop the "man" when referring to both men & women	
	Refrain from stereotyping jobs and social roles by gender	
	Use names that groups use to identify themselves	

Section V English Chat Tasks

1. Q&A (5 questions): Work in groups to ask and answer questions prepared in the

pre-class task.

2. A complete speech includes an introduction, main body and conclusion (Table 13.3). There are many techniques a speaker can use to create these parts of a speech. Discuss in groups what specific techniques the speaker uses in this speech and write down your answers.

Table 13.3 Sections and Techniques of the Speech (13)

Sections of a Speech	Techniques Used in a Speech	Techniques the Speaker Uses in the Speech
Introduction	1. Relate the topic to the audience 2. State the importance of your topic 3. Startle the audience 4. Arouse the curiosity of the audience 5. Question the audience 6. Begin with a quotation 7. Tell a story	
Main body	1. Evidence and examples 2. Explanation and analysis 3. Visual aids 4. Personal stories or anecdotes 5. Expert opinions or quotes 6. Transitions	
Conclusion	1. Signal the end of the speech 2. Summarize the speech 3. End with a quotation 4. Make a dramatic statement 5. Refer to the introduction	

Section VI EANLIC Party Tasks

1. Group Work

In groups, research an inspirational role model honored in annual Touching China Awards and deliver a speech about their life and achievements.

2. Prepared Speech

Three students will deliver prepared speeches each week. Score their work according to the feedback checklist below (Table 13.4).

Table 13.4　Checklist（13）

Checklist	Speech 1 1–5 From the least to the most	Speech 2 1–5 From the least to the most	Speech 3 1–5 From the least to the most
Is the speech well-prepared?	1　2　3　4　5	1　2　3　4　5	1　2　3　4　5
Was the speaker's voice loud enough?	1　2　3　4　5	1　2　3　4　5	1　2　3　4　5
Did the speaker look at the audience?	1　2　3　4　5	1　2　3　4　5	1　2　3　4　5
Did the speaker look confident?	1　2　3　4　5	1　2　3　4　5	1　2　3　4　5
Was there a clear and logical structure in the speech?	1　2　3　4　5	1　2　3　4　5	1　2　3　4　5
Were all the major claims supported by evidence?	1　2　3　4　5	1　2　3　4　5	1　2　3　4　5
Have you found any mistakes in grammar/pronunciation?			
Do you have any suggestions for the speaker to improve next time?			

3. Debate

Directions: *Work in groups to prepare a claim or counterclaim for the following idea beforehand, and then participate in the debate at the EANLIC Party.*

Some people look at our challenges and our limitations as something negative or bad, while others look at them as blessings, magnificent gifts.

4. Activities Focusing on Words and Expressions

Design an activity using words and expressions from the speech.

Section VII　Assignment

Prepare a speech on "If your life were a book and you were the author, how would you want your story to go?".

● Make sure the language you use in your speech is accurately, clearly, appropriately and inclusively.

● Ensure that your speech is well-expressed and engaging.

Unit 14 How to Gain Control of Your Free Time

By Laura Vanderkam

Learning Objectives

1. Achieve a thorough understanding of the speech contextually and linguistically.
2. Learn to express yourselves more freely on the topic of time management.
3. Be able to use vivid language in a public speech.
4. Improve time management skills.

Text

When people find out I write about time management, they assume two things. *One is that I'm always on time, and I'm not.* I have four small children, and I would like to blame them for my occasional tardiness, but sometimes it's just not their fault. I was once late to my own speech on time management.

We all had to just take a moment together and savor that irony.

The second thing they assume is that *I have lots of tips and tricks for saving bits of time here and there.* Sometimes I'll hear from magazines that are doing a story along these lines, generally on how to help their readers find an extra hour in the day. And the idea is that we'll shave bits of time off everyday activities, add it up, and we'll have time for the good stuff. I question the entire premise of this piece, but I'm always interested in hearing what they've come up with before they call me. Some of my favorites: doing errands where you only have to make right-hand turns.

Being extremely judicious in microwave usage: it says three to three-and-a-half minutes on the package, we're totally getting in on the bottom side of that. And my personal favorite, which makes sense on some level, is to DVR your favorite shows so you can fast-forward through the commercials. That way, you save eight minutes every half hour, so in the course of two hours of watching TV, you find 32 minutes to exercise.

Which is true. You know another way to find 32 minutes to exercise? Don't watch two hours of TV a day, right?

Anyway, the idea is we'll save bits of time here and there, add it up, and we will finally get to everything we want to do. But after studying how successful people spend their time and looking at their schedules hour by hour, I think this idea has it completely backward. *We don't build the lives we want by saving time. We build the lives we want, and then time saves itself.*

Here's what I mean. *I recently did a time diary project looking at 1,001 days in the lives of extremely busy women.* They had demanding jobs, sometimes their own businesses, kids to care for, maybe parents to care for, community commitments—busy, busy people. I had them keep track of their time for a week so I could add up how much they worked and slept, and I interviewed them about their strategies, for my book.

One of the women whose time log I studied goes out on a Wednesday night for something. She comes home to find that her water heater has broken, and there is now water all over her basement. If you've ever had anything like this happen to you, you know it is a hugely damaging, frightening, sopping mess. So she's dealing with the immediate aftermath that night, next day she's got plumbers coming in, day after that, professional cleaning crew dealing with the ruined carpet. All this is being recorded on her time log. Winds up taking seven hours of her week. Seven hours. That's like finding an extra hour in the day.

But I'm sure if you had asked her at the start of the week, "Could you find seven hours to train for a triathlon?" "Could you find seven hours to mentor seven worthy people?" I'm sure she would've said what most of us would've said, which is, "No—can't you see how busy I am?" Yet when she had to find seven hours because there is water all over her basement, she found seven hours. And what this shows us is that time is highly elastic. We cannot make more time, but time will stretch to accommodate what we choose to put into it.

And *so the key to time management is treating our priorities as the equivalent of that broken water heater.* To get at this, I like to use language from one of the busiest people I ever interviewed. By busy, I mean she was running a small business with 12 people on the payroll. She had six children in her spare time. I was getting in touch with her to set up an interview on how she "had it all"—that phrase. I remember it was a Thursday morning, and she was not available to speak with me. Of course, right?

But the reason she was unavailable to speak with me is that she was out for a hike, because it was a beautiful spring morning, and she wanted to go for a hike. So of course this makes me even more intrigued, and when I finally do catch up with her, she explains it like this. She says, "Listen, Laura, everything I do, every minute I spend, is my choice." And rather than say, "I don't have time to do x, y or z," she'd say, "I don't do x, y or z because it's not a priority." "I don't have time," often means "It's not a priority." If you think about it, that's really more accurate language. I could tell you I don't have time to dust my blinds, but that's not true. If you offered to pay me $100,000 to dust my blinds, I would get to it pretty quickly.

Since that is not going to happen, I can acknowledge this is not a matter of lacking time; it's that I don't want to do it. Using this language reminds us that time is a choice. And granted, there may be horrible consequences for making different choices, I will give you that. But we are smart people, and certainly over the long run, we have the power to fill our lives with the things that deserve to be there.

So how do we do that? How do we treat *our priorities as the* equivalent of that broken water heater?

Well, first we need to figure out what they are. I want to give you two strategies for thinking about this. The first, on the professional side: I'm sure many people coming up to the end of the year are giving or getting annual performance reviews. You look back over your successes over the year, your "opportunities for growth". And this serves its purpose, but I find it's more effective to do this looking forward. So I want you to pretend it's the end of next year. You're giving yourself a performance review, and it has been an absolutely amazing year for you professionally. What three to five things did you do that made it so amazing? So you can write next year's performance review now.

And you can do this for your personal life, too. I'm sure many of you, like me, come December, get cards that contain these folded up sheets of colored paper, on which is written what is known as the family holiday letter.

Bit of a wretched genre of literature, really, going on about how amazing everyone in the household is, or even more scintillating, how busy everyone in the household is. But these letters serve a purpose, which is that they tell your friends and family what you did in your personal life that mattered to you over the year. So this year's kind of done, but I want you to pretend it's the end of next year, and it has been an absolutely amazing year for you and the people you care about. What three to five things did you do that made it so amazing? So you can write next year's family holiday letter now. Don't send it.

Please, don't send it. But you can write it. And now, between the performance review and the family holiday letter, we have a list of six to ten goals we can work on in the next year.

And now we need to break these down into doable steps. So maybe you want to write a family history. First, you can read some other family histories, get a sense for the style. Then maybe think about the questions you want to ask your relatives, set up appointments to interview them. Or maybe you want to run a 5K. So you need to find a race and sign up, figure out a training plan, and dig those shoes out of the back of the closet. And then—this is key—we treat our priorities as the equivalent of that broken water heater, by putting them into our schedules first. We do this by thinking through our weeks before we are in them.

I find a really good time to do this is Friday afternoons. Friday afternoon is what an economist might call a "low opportunity cost" time. Most of us are not sitting there on Friday afternoons saying, "I am excited to make progress toward my personal and professional priorities right now."

But we are willing to think about what those should be. So take a little bit of time Friday afternoon, make yourself a three-category priority list: *career*, *relationships*, *self*. Making a three-category list reminds us that there should be something in all three categories. Career, we think about; relationships, self—not so much. But anyway, just a short list, two to three items in each. Then look out over the whole of the next week, and see where you can plan them in.

Where you plan them in is up to you. I know this is going to be more complicated for some people than others. I mean, some people's lives are just harder than others. It is not going to be easy to find time to take that poetry class if you are caring for multiple children on your own. I get that. And I don't want to minimize anyone's struggle. But I do think that the numbers I am about to tell you are empowering.

There are 168 hours in a week. Twenty-four times seven is 168 hours. That is a lot of time. If you are working a full-time job, so 40 hours a week, sleeping eight hours a night, so 56 hours a week—that leaves 72 hours for other things. That is a lot of time. You say you're working 50 hours a week, maybe a main job and a side hustle. Well, that leaves 62 hours for other things. You say you're working 60 hours. Well, that leaves 52 hours for other things. You say you're working more than 60 hours. Well, are you sure?

There was once a study comparing people's estimated work weeks with time diaries. They found that people claiming 75-plus-hour work weeks were off by about 25 hours.

You can guess in which direction, right? Anyway, in 168 hours a week, I think we can *find time for what matters to you.* If you want to spend more time with your kids, you want to study more for a test you're taking, you want to exercise for three hours and volunteer for two, you can. And that's even if you're working way more than full-time hours.

So we have plenty of time, which is great, because guess what? We don't even need that much time to do amazing things. But when most of us have bits of time, what do we do? Pull out the phone, right? Start deleting emails. Otherwise, we're puttering around the house or watching TV.

But small moments can have great power. You can use your bits of time for bits of joy. Maybe it's choosing to read something wonderful on the bus on the way to work. I know when I had a job that required two bus rides and a subway ride every morning, I used to go to the library on weekends to get stuff to read. It made the whole experience almost, almost, enjoyable. Breaks at work can be used for meditating or praying. If family dinner is out because of your crazy work schedule, maybe family breakfast could be a good substitute.

It's about looking at the whole of one's time and seeing where the good stuff can go. I truly believe this. There is time. *Even if we are busy, we have time for what matters. And when we focus on what matters, we can build the lives we want in the time we've got.*

Thank you.

Section I Pre-class Tasks

Directions: *Finish the following tasks before class.*

1. Watch and listen to the speech for the first time, and get the main idea of the speech.

2. Watch the speech for the second time and find the answers to the following questions.

（1）What is your definition of free time?

（2）What is a family holiday letter?

（3）What is your understanding of "Time is a choice"?

（4）Do you agree/disagree with the speaker's idea? Why or why not?

（5）Identify and underline metaphor, parallelism, repetition, and opposition used in the speech.

3. Design 5 open-ended questions to interview five other students at the English chat. Write down your questions and peer evaluation in Table 14.1.

Table 14.1　Questions and Peer Evaluation (14)

Questions	Peer Evaluation (appropriateness, grammatical accuracy)
1.	
2.	
3.	
4.	
5.	
Student evaluator signature	

Section II　Language Focus

1. Words & Expressions

- **tardiness** /ˈtɑːdɪnəs/　*n.* the quality or habit of not adhering to a correct or usual or expected time 拖拉；缓慢；迟缓

- **premise** /ˈpremɪs/　*n.* a statement or an idea that forms the basis for a reasonable line of argument 前提；假定

- **judicious** /dʒuˈdɪʃəs/　*adj.* careful and sensible; showing good judgement 审慎而明智的；明断的；有见地的

- **log** /lɒɡ/　*n.* a log is an official written account of what happens each day, for example on board a ship (航海等的) 日志；日记

- **sopping** /ˈsɒpɪŋ/　*adj.* extremely wet 湿透的；湿漉漉的

- **plumber** /ˈplʌmə(r)/　*n.* a person whose job is to fit and repair things such as water pipes, toilets, etc. 水暖工；管子工

- **elastic** /ɪˈlæstɪk/　*adj.* something that is elastic is able to stretch easily and then return to its original size and shape 有弹性的；有弹力的

- **accommodate** /əˈkɒmədeɪt/　*v.* to make fit for, or change to suit a new purpose 顺应；适应（新情况）

- **priority** /praɪˈɒrəti/　*n.* something that you think is more important than other things and should be dealt with first 优先事项；最重要的事；首要事情

- **equivalent** /ɪˈkwɪvələnt/　*n.* a person or thing equal to another in value or measure or

force or effect or significance, etc. 相等的东西；等量；对应词
- **intrigued** /ɪnˈtriːgd/ *adj.* very interested in sth./sb. and wanting to know more about it/them 着迷；很感兴趣；好奇
- **dust** /dʌst/ *v.* to remove the dust from 擦去……的灰尘；掸去；擦去
- **blind** /blaɪnd/ *n.* a covering for a window, especially one made of a roll of cloth that is fixed at the top of the window and can be pulled up and down 窗帘；（尤指）卷帘
- **acknowledge** /əkˈnɒlɪdʒ/ *v.* to accept that sth. is true 承认（权威、地位）；承认（属实）
- **wretched** /ˈretʃɪd/ *adj.* making you feel sympathy or pity; feeling ill/sick or unhappy 可怜的，悲惨的；感到不适的；难受的；不愉快的
- **genre** /ˈʒɒ̃rə/ *n.* a particular type or style of literature, art, film or music that you can recognize because of its special features （文学、艺术、电影或音乐的）体裁；类型
- **scintillating** /ˈsɪntɪleɪtɪŋ/ *adj.* very clever, amusing and interesting 才情洋溢的；妙趣横生的
- **minimize** /ˈmɪnɪmaɪz/ *v.* to try to make sth. seem less important than it really is 降低；贬低；使显得不重要
- **putter** /ˈpʌtə(r)/ *v.* if you putter around, you do unimportant but quite enjoyable things, without hurrying 慢条斯理地工作；悠然自得地做
- **meditate** /ˈmedɪteɪt/ *v.* to think intently and at length, as for spiritual purposes 冥想；沉思
- **substitute** /ˈsʌbstɪtjuːt/ *n.* a person or thing that you use or have instead of the one you normally use or have 代用品；代替者；代替物

2. **Sentences for Further Understanding**

   Directions: *Translate the following sentences from English into Chinese.*

- Being extremely judicious in microwave usage: it says three to three-and-a-half minutes on the package, we're totally getting in on the bottom side of that.
- But after studying how successful people spend their time and looking at their schedules hour by hour, I think this idea has it completely backward.
- We don't build the lives we want by saving time. We build the lives we want, and then time saves itself.
- If you've ever had anything like this happen to you, you know it is a hugely damaging, frightening, sopping mess.

- What this shows us is that time is highly elastic. We cannot make more time, but time will stretch to accommodate what we choose to put into it.
- So the key to time management is treating our priorities as the equivalent of that broken water heater.
- She says, "Listen, Laura, everything I do, every minute I spend, is my choice."
- If you offered to pay me $100,000 to dust my blinds, I would get to it pretty quickly.
- Since that is not going to happen, I can acknowledge this is not a matter of lacking time; it's that I don't want to do it.
- We are smart people, and certainly over the long run, we have the power to fill our lives with the things that deserve to be there.
- Friday afternoon is what an economist might call a "low opportunity cost" time.
- But small moments can have great power. You can use your bits of time for bits of joy.
- When we focus on what matters, we can build the lives we want in the time we've got.

Section III Outline of the Speech

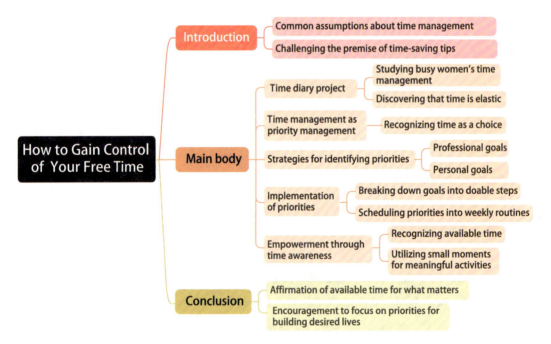

Section IV Public Speaking Skills

Using language vividly helps bring your speech to life. One way to make your language more vivid is through imagery, which you can develop by using concrete language, simile and metaphor. Another way to make your language vivid is by exploiting the rhythm of language with parallelism, repetition, alliteration, and antithesis. Here are some tips on how to use language vividly in a speech (Table 14.1).

Table 14.1 Tips on How to Use Language Vividly

Tips		How to Use Language Vividly
Imagery	Concrete words	Words that represent tangible, physical objects that can be perceived through the senses, such as touch, sight, taste, hearing, or smell
		eg. water, tree, apple, car, etc.
	Simile	A figure of speech that involves comparing two different things using the words "like" or "as" to highlight a shared characteristic or quality
		eg. His smile was like sunshine.
	Metaphor	A figure of speech that involves making a direct comparison between two unrelated things, suggesting that they are alike in some way
		eg. Time is a thief.
Rhythm	Parallelism	A rhetorical device or literary technique in which parts of a sentence or multiple sentences are grammatically or structurally similar in construction
		eg. Grit is passion and perseverance for a very long-time goal. Grit is having stamina. Grit is sticking with your future, day in and day out.
	Repetition	A literary device that involves the repeated use of words, phrases, sounds, or other elements in a speech, writing, or work of art
		eg. We must imagine greatly, dare greatly, and act greatly.
	Alliteration	A literary device characterized by the repetition of the initial consonant sounds in a sequence of words within close proximity
		eg. She sells seashells by the seashore.
	Antithesis	A rhetorical device that involves the juxtaposition of contrasting ideas, words, phrases, or sentences within a parallel grammatical structure
		eg. Ask not what your country can do for you; ask what you can do for your country.

Section V English Chat Tasks

1. Q&A (5 questions): Work in groups to ask and answer questions prepared in the

pre-class task.

2. A complete speech includes an introduction, main body and conclusion (Table 14.2). There are many techniques a speaker can use to create these parts of a speech. Discuss in groups what specific techniques the speaker uses in this speech and write down your answers.

Table 14.2 Sections and Techniques of the Speech (14)

Sections of a Speech	Techniques Used in a Speech	Techniques the Speaker Uses in the Speech
Introduction	1. Relate the topic to the audience 2. State the importance of your topic 3. Startle the audience 4. Arouse the curiosity of the audience 5. Question the audience 6. Begin with a quotation 7. Tell a story	
Main body	1. Evidence and examples 2. Explanation and analysis 3. Visual aids 4. Personal stories or anecdotes 5. Expert opinions or quotes 6. Transitions	
Conclusion	1. Signal the end of the speech 2. Summarize the speech 3. End with a quotation 4. Make a dramatic statement 5. Refer to the introduction	

Section VI EANLIC Party Tasks

1. Group Work

In groups, research an inspirational role model honored in annual Touching China Awards and deliver a speech about their life and achievements.

2. Prepared Speech

Three students will deliver prepared speeches each week. Score their work according to the feedback checklist below (Table 14.3).

Table 14.3 Checklist (14)

Checklist	Speech 1 1–5 From the least to the most	Speech 2 1–5 From the least to the most	Speech 3 1–5 From the least to the most
Is the speech well-prepared?	1 2 3 4 5	1 2 3 4 5	1 2 3 4 5
Was the speaker's voice loud enough?	1 2 3 4 5	1 2 3 4 5	1 2 3 4 5
Did the speaker look at the audience?	1 2 3 4 5	1 2 3 4 5	1 2 3 4 5
Did the speaker look confident?	1 2 3 4 5	1 2 3 4 5	1 2 3 4 5
Was there a clear and logical structure in the speech?	1 2 3 4 5	1 2 3 4 5	1 2 3 4 5
Were all the major claims supported by evidence?	1 2 3 4 5	1 2 3 4 5	1 2 3 4 5
Have you found any mistakes in grammar/pronunciation?			
Do you have any suggestions for the speaker to improve next time?			

3. Debate

Directions: *Work in groups to prepare a claim or counterclaim for the following idea beforehand, and then participate in the debate at the EANLIC Party.*

Some people think that time can be saved from daily chores, while others think that time is a choice.

4. Activities Focusing on Words and Expressions

Design an activity using words and expressions from the speech.

Section VII Assignment

Make a three-category priority list: study, relationship and self, three items in each.

Share your priority list with your classmates. Tell them what your priorities are and why you put them in the list.

Unit 15 How AI Could Save (Not Destroy) Education

By Sal Khan

Learning Objectives

1. Achieve a thorough understanding of the speech contextually and linguistically.
2. Learn to express yourselves more freely on the topic of AI.
3. Use visual aids properly in a speech.
4. Recognize the crucial role AI plays in education and use it rationally and ethically.

Text

So anyone who's been paying attention for the last few months has been seeing headlines like this, especially in education. The thesis has been: students are going to be using ChatGPT and other forms of AI to cheat, do their assignments. They're not going to learn. And it's going to completely undermine education as we know it.

Now, what I'm going to argue today is not only are there ways to mitigate all of that—if we put the right *guardrails*, we do the right things, we can mitigate it, but I think we're at the cusp of using AI for probably the biggest positive transformation that education has ever seen. And *the way we're going to do that is by giving every student on the planet an artificially intelligent but amazing personal tutor.* And we're going to give every teacher on the planet an amazing, artificially intelligent teaching assistant.

And just to appreciate how big of a deal it would be to give everyone a personal tutor, I show you this clip from Benjamin Bloom's 1984 2 sigma study, or he called it the "2 sigma problem". The 2 sigma comes from two standard deviations, sigma, the symbol for standard deviation. And he had good data that showed that look, a normal distribution, that's the one that you see in the traditional bell curve right in the middle, that's how the world kind of sorts itself out, that if you were to give personal 1-to-1 to tutoring for students, then you could actually get a distribution that looks like that right. It says tutorial 1-to-1 with the asterisks, like, that right distribution, a two standard-deviation improvement.

Just to put that in plain language, that could take your average student and turn them into an exceptional student. It can take your below-average student and turn them into an above-average student.

Now the reason why he framed it as a problem, was he said, well, this is all good, but how do you actually scale group instruction this way? How do you actually give it to everyone in an economic way?

What I'm about to show you is I think the first moves towards doing that. Obviously, we've been trying to approximate it in some way at Khan Academy for over a decade now, but I think we're at the cusp of accelerating it dramatically. *I'm going to show you the early stages of what our AI, which we call Khanmigo, what it can now do and maybe a little bit of where it is actually going.*

So this right over here is a traditional exercise that you or many of your children might have seen on Khan Academy. But what's new is that little bot thing at the right. And we'll start by seeing one of the very important safeguards, which is the conversation is recorded and viewable by your teacher. It's moderated actually by a second AI. And also it does not tell you the answer. It is not a cheating tool. When the student says, "Tell me the answer," it says, "I'm your tutor. What do you think is the next step for solving the problem?"

Now, if the student makes a mistake, and this will surprise people who think large language models are not good at mathematics, notice, not only does it notice the mistake, it asks the student to explain their reasoning, but it's actually doing what I would say, not just even an average tutor would do, but an excellent tutor would do. It's able to divine what is probably the misconception in that student's mind, that they probably didn't use the distributive property. Remember, we need to distribute the negative two to both the nine and the 2 m inside of the parentheses. This to me is a very, very, very big deal. And it's not just in math.

This is a computer programming exercise on Khan Academy, where the student needs to make the clouds part. And so we can see the student starts defining a variable, left X minus minus. It only made the left cloud part. But then they can ask Khanmigo, what's going on? Why is only the left cloud moving? And it understands the code. It knows all the context of what the student is doing, and it understands that those ellipses are there to draw clouds, which I think is kind of mind-blowing. And it says, "To make the right cloud move as well, try adding a line of code inside the draw function that increments the right X variable by one pixel in each frame."

Now, this one is maybe even more amazing because we have a lot of math teachers. We've all been trying to teach the world to code, but there aren't a lot of computing teachers out there. And what you just saw, even when I'm tutoring my kids, when they're learning to code, I can't help them this well, this fast, *this is really going to be a super tutor.*

And it's not just exercises. It understands what you're watching. It understands the context of your video. It can answer the age-old question, "Why do I need to learn this?" And it asks Socratically, "Well, what do you care about?" And let's say the student says, "I want to be a professional athlete." And it says, "Well, learning about the size of cells, which is what this video is, that could be really useful for understanding nutrition and how your body works, etc." It can answer questions. It can quiz you. It can connect it to other ideas. You can now ask as many questions of a video as you could ever dream of.

Another big shortage out there—I remember the high school I went to, the student-to-guidance counselor ratio was about 200 or 300 to one. A lot of the country, it's worse than that. We can use Khanmigo to give every student a guidance counselor, academic coach, career coach, life coach, which is exactly what you see right over here. And we launched this with the GPT-4 launch. We have a few thousand people on this. This isn't a fake demo; this is really it in action.

And then there is, you know, things that I think it would have been even harder. It would have been a little science fiction to do with even a traditional tutor. We run an online high school with Arizona State University called Khan World School, and we have a student who attends that online school based in India. Her name's Saanvi. And she was doing a report on *The Great Gatsby*. And when she was reading *The Great Gatsby*, Jay Gatsby keeps looking at the green light off into the distance. And she's like, "Why does he do that?" She did some web searches, and people have obviously studied this and commented about the symbolism of that, but none of it was really resonating with her. And then she realized that she had Khanmigo and that she could talk to Jay Gatsby himself.

And so, "Ah, splendid choice, old sport. I am now Jay Gatsby, the enigmatic millionaire from F. Scott Fitzgerald's classic."

And so, "Why do you keep staring at the green light?"

"Ah, the green light, old sport. It's a symbol of my dreams and desires, you see. It's situated at the end of Daisy Buchanan's dock across the bay from my mansion. I gaze at it longingly as it represents my yearning for the past and my hope to reunite with Daisy, the love of my life."

And what was cool is, Saanvi then said, "I had this long conversation," she called him "Mr. Gatsby", and at the end she actually apologized for taking his time, which I thought was very polite of her.

But you can imagine this unlocks learning literature, learning ... You could talk to historical figures. We're even probably going to add an activity you can talk to like, the Mississippi River. It brings things to life in ways that really were science fiction even six months or a year ago.

Students can get into debates with the AI. And we've got this here is the student debating whether we should cancel student debt. The student is against canceling student debt, and we've gotten very clear feedback. We started running it at Khan World School in our lab school that we have, Khan Lab School. The students, the high school students especially, they're saying, "This is amazing to be able to fine-tune my arguments without fearing judgment. It makes me that much more confident to go into the classroom and really participate." And we all know that Socratic dialogue debate is a great way to learn, but frankly, it's not out there for most students. But now it can be accessible to hopefully everyone.

A lot of the narrative, we saw that in the headlines, has been, "It's going to do the writing for kids. Kids are not going to learn to write." *But we are showing that there are ways that the AI doesn't write for you, it writes with you.*

So this is a little thing, and my eight year old is addicted to this, and he's not a kid that really liked writing before, but you can say, "I want to write a horror story," and it says, "Ooh, a horror story, how spine-tingling and thrilling! Let's dive into the world of eerie shadows and chilling mysteries." And this is an activity where the student will write two sentences, and then the AI will write two sentences. And so they collaborate together on a story.

The student writes, "Beatrice was a misunderstood ghost. She wanted to make friends but kept scaring them by accident."

And the AI says, "Poor Beatrice, a lonely spirit yearning for companionship. One day she stumbled upon an old abandoned mansion," etc.

I encourage you all to hopefully one day try this. This is surprisingly fun.

Now to even more directly hit this use case. And what I'm about to show you, everything I showed you so far is actually already part of Khanmigo, and what I'm about to show you, we haven't shown to anyone yet, this is a prototype. We hope to be able to launch it in the next few months, but this is to directly use AI, use generative AI, to not undermine English and language arts but to actually enhance it in ways that we couldn't have even conceived of even a year ago. This is reading comprehension. The students reading Steve Jobs's famous speech at Stanford. And then as they get to certain points, they can click on that little question. And the AI will then Socratically, almost like an oral exam, ask the student about things. And the AI can highlight parts of the passage. Why did the author use that word? What was their intent? Does it back up their argument? They can start to do stuff that once again, we never had the capability to give everyone a tutor, everyone a writing coach to actually dig in to reading at this level.

And you could go on the other side of it. And we have whole work flows that helps them write, helps them be a writing coach, draw an outline. But once a student actually constructs a draft, and this is where they're constructing a draft, they can ask for feedback once again, as you would expect from a good writing coach. In this case, the student will say, let's say, "Does my evidence support my claim?" And then the AI, not only is able to give feedback, but it's able to highlight certain parts of the passage and says, "On this passage, this doesn't quite support your claim," but once again, Socratically says, "Can you tell us why?" So it's pulling the student, making them a better writer, giving them far more feedback than they've ever been able to actually get before. And we think this is going to dramatically accelerate writing, not hurt it.

Now, everything I've talked about so far is for the student. *But we think this could be equally as powerful for the teacher to drive more personalized education and frankly save time and energy for themselves and for their students.* So this is an American history exercise on Khan Academy. It's a question about the Spanish-American War. And at first it's in student mode. And if you say, "Tell me the answer," it's not going to tell the answer. It's going to go into tutoring mode. But that little toggle which teachers have access to, they can turn student mode off and then it goes into teacher mode. And what this does is it turns into—you could view it as a teacher's guide on steroids. Not only can it explain the answer, it can explain how you might want to teach it. It can help prepare the teacher for that material. It can help them create lesson plans, as you could see doing right there. It'll eventually help them create progress reports and help them, eventually, grade. So once again, teachers spend about half their time with this type of activity, lesson planning. All of that energy can go back to them or go back to human interactions with their actual students.

So, you know, one point I want to make. These large language models are so powerful, there's a temptation to say like, well, all these people are just going to slap them onto their websites, and it kind of turns the applications themselves into commodities. And what I've got to tell you is that's one of the reasons why I didn't sleep for two weeks when I first had access to GPT-4 back in August. But we quickly realized that to actually make it magical, I think what you saw with Khanmigo a little bit, it didn't interact with you the way that you see ChatGPT interacting. It was a little bit more magical. It was more Socratic. It was clearly much better at math than what most people are used to thinking. And the reason is, there was a lot of work behind the scenes to make that happen.

And I could go through the whole list of everything we've been working on, many, many people for over six, seven months to make it feel magical. But perhaps the most intellectually interesting one is we realized, and this was an idea from an OpenAI researcher, that we could dramatically improve its ability in math and its ability in tutoring if we allow the AI to think before it speaks. So if you're tutoring someone and you immediately just start talking before you assess their math, you might not get it right. But if you construct thoughts for yourself, and what you see on the right there is an actual AI thought, something that it generates for itself but it does not share with the student. then its accuracy went up dramatically, and its ability to be a world-class tutor went up dramatically. And you can see it's talking to itself here. It says, "The student got a different answer than I did, but do not tell them they made a mistake. Instead, ask them to explain how they got to that step."

So I'll just finish off, hopefully, you know, what I've just shown you is just half of what we are working on, and we think this is just the very tip of the iceberg of where this can actually go. And I'm pretty convinced, which I wouldn't have been even a year ago, that we together have a chance of addressing the 2 sigma problem and turning it into a 2 sigma opportunity, dramatically accelerating education as we know it.

Now, just to take a step back at a meta level, obviously we heard a lot today, the debates on either side. There are folks who take a more pessimistic view of AI. They say this is scary; there are all these dystopian scenarios; we maybe want to slow down; we want to pause. On the other side, there are the more optimistic folks that say, well, we've gone through inflection points before, we've gone through the Industrial

Revolution. It was scary, but it all kind of worked out. And what I'd argue right now is I don't think this is like a flip of a coin or this is something where we'll just have to, like, wait and see which way it turns out. I think everyone here and beyond; we are active participants in this decision. I'm pretty convinced that the first line of reasoning is actually almost a self-fulfilling prophecy, that if we act with fear and if we say, "Hey, we've just got to stop doing this stuff," what's really going to happen is the rule followers might pause, might slow down, but the rule breakers, as Alexander [Wang] mentioned, the totalitarian governments, the criminal organizations, they're only going to accelerate. And that leads to what I am pretty convinced is the dystopian state, which is the good actors have worse AIs than the bad actors.

But I'll also, you know, talk to the optimists a little bit. I don't think that means that, oh, yeah, then we should just relax and just hope for the best. That might not happen either. *I think all of us together have to fight like hell to make sure that we put the guardrails, we put in—when the problems arise—reasonable regulations.* But we fight like hell for the positive use cases. Because very close to my heart, and obviously there are many potential positive use cases, but perhaps the most powerful use case and perhaps the most poetic use case is *if AI, artificial intelligence, can be used to enhance HI, human intelligence, human potential and human purpose.*

Thank you.

Section I Pre-class Tasks

Directions: *Finish the following tasks before class.*

1. Watch and listen to the speech for the first time, and get the main idea of the speech.

2. Watch the speech for the second time and find the answers to the following questions.

(1) What is AI?

(2) According to the speaker, how does AI save education?

(3) How does AI help students with writing?

(4) Why does the speaker say that AI is an amazing teaching assistant?

(5) What kind of visual aids are used in the speech?

3. Design 5 open-ended questions to interview five other students at the English chat. Write down your questions and peer evaluation in Table 15.1.

Table 15.1 Questions and Peer Evaluation (15)

Questions	Peer Evaluation (appropriateness, grammatical accuracy)
1.	
2.	
3.	
4.	
5.	
Student evaluator signature	

Section II Language Focus

1. Words & Expressions

- **undermine** /ˌʌndəˈmaɪn/ *v.* if you undermine sth. such as a feeling or a system, you make it less strong or less secure than it was before, often by a gradual process or by repeated efforts（常指间接地）削弱；损害；动摇（某人的地位或权威）

- **mitigate** /ˈmɪtɪɡeɪt/ *v.* to make sth. less harmful, serious, etc. 减轻；缓解；缓和

- **cusp** /kʌsp/ *n.* if you say that sb. or sth. is on the cusp, you mean they are between two states, or are about to be in a particular state 介于两个状态之间；即将进入特定状态

- **deviation** /ˌdiːviˈeɪʃn/ *n.* the amount by which a single measurement is different from the average 偏差

- **asterisk** /ˈæstərɪsk/ *n.* the symbol (*) placed next to a particular word or phrase to make people notice it or to show that more information is given in another place 星号（置于词语旁以引起注意或另有注释）

- **exceptional** /ɪkˈsepʃənl/ *adj.* unusually good 杰出的；优秀的；卓越的

- **ellipse** /ɪˈlɪps/ *n.* a regular oval shape, like a circle that has been squeezed on two sides 椭圆；椭圆形

- **increment** /ˈɪŋkrəmənt/ *n.* an increase in a number or an amount 增量；增加

- **variable** /ˈveəriəbl/ *n.* a situation, number or quantity that can vary or be varied 可变情况；变量；可变因素

- **enigmatic** /ˌenɪɡˈmætɪk/ *adj.* mysterious and difficult to understand 神秘的；费解的；令人困惑的

- **spine-tingling** /ˈspaɪn tɪŋɡlɪŋ/ *adj.* enjoyable because it is very exciting or frightening

紧张刺激的；惊险的

- **eerie** /ˈɪəri/ *adj.* inspiring a feeling of fear 怪异的；诡异的
- **stumble** /ˈstʌmbl/ *v.* to miss a step and fall or nearly fall 绊倒
- **generative** /ˈdʒenərətɪv/ *adj.* if sth. is generative, it is capable of producing sth. or causing it to develop 能生产的；有生产能力的；促使……生成的
- **toggle** /ˈtɒɡl/ *n.* a key on a computer that you press to change from one style or operation to another, and back again 转换键；切换键
- **steroid** /ˈsterɔɪd/ *n.* any hormone affecting the development and growth of sex organs 类固醇；甾族化合物
- **commodity** /kəˈmɒdəti/ *n.* a product or a raw material that can be bought and sold 商品；有用的东西；有使用价值的事物
- **pessimistic** /ˌpesɪˈmɪstɪk/ *adj.* expecting bad things to happen or sth. not to be successful; showing pessimism 悲观的；悲观主义的

2. Sentences for Further Understanding

Directions: *Translate the following sentences from English into Chinese.*

- Now, what I'm going to argue today is not only are there ways to mitigate all of that—if we put the right guardrails, we do the right things, we can mitigate it.
- I think we're at the cusp of using AI for probably the biggest positive transformation that education has ever seen.
- Just to put that in plain language, that could take your average student and turn them into an exceptional student. It can take your below-average student and turn them into an above-average student.
- I gaze at it longingly as it represents my yearning for the past and my hope to reunite with Daisy, the love of my life.
- So it's pulling the student, making them a better writer, giving them far more feedback than they've ever been able to actually get before.
- We think this could be equally as powerful for the teacher to drive more personalized education and frankly save time and energy for themselves and for their students.
- What I'd argue right now is I don't think this is like a flip of a coin or this is something where we'll just have to, like, wait and see which way it turns out.
- I think everyone here and beyond; we are active participants in this decision.
- I think all of us together have to fight like hell to make sure that we put the guardrails, we put in—when the problems arise—reasonable regulations.

- The most powerful use case and perhaps the most poetic use case is if AI, artificial intelligence, can be used to enhance HI, human intelligence, human potential and human purpose.

Section III Outline of the Speech

How AI Could Save (Not Destroy) Education

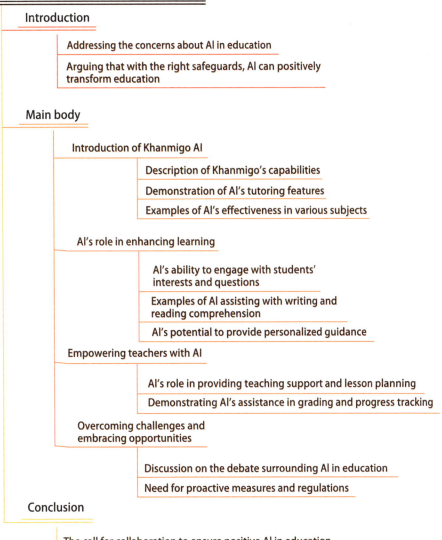

- Introduction
  - Addressing the concerns about AI in education
  - Arguing that with the right safeguards, AI can positively transform education
- Main body
  - Introduction of Khanmigo AI
    - Description of Khanmigo's capabilities
    - Demonstration of AI's tutoring features
    - Examples of AI's effectiveness in various subjects
  - AI's role in enhancing learning
    - AI's ability to engage with students' interests and questions
    - Examples of AI assisting with writing and reading comprehension
    - AI's potential to provide personalized guidance
  - Empowering teachers with AI
    - AI's role in providing teaching support and lesson planning
    - Demonstrating AI's assistance in grading and progress tracking
  - Overcoming challenges and embracing opportunities
    - Discussion on the debate surrounding AI in education
    - Need for proactive measures and regulations
- Conclusion
  - The call for collaboration to ensure positive AI in education
  - Using AI to empower education, enhance human intelligence, potential, and purpose

Section IV Public Speaking Skills

Visual aids are tools or materials that complement a verbal presentation to enhance audience's understanding and retention of information. They can take various forms, such as slides, charts, graphs, props, models, videos, or images. The primary purpose of visual aids is to make your speech more engaging, memorable, and easier to comprehend. Here are some common types of visual aids and tips on how to apply them effectively in a speech.

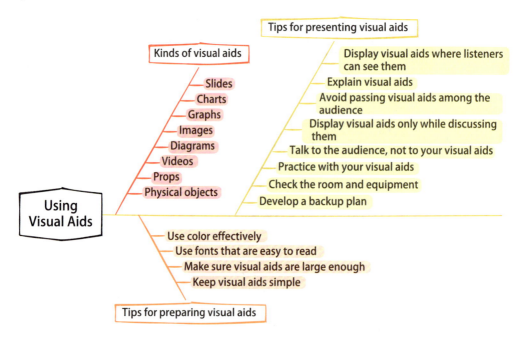

Section V English Chat Tasks

1. Q&A (5 questions): Work in groups to ask and answer questions prepared in the pre-class task.

2. A complete speech includes an introduction, main body and conclusion (Table 15.2). There are many techniques a speaker can use to create these parts of a speech. Discuss in groups what specific techniques the speaker uses in this speech and write down your answers.

Table 15.2 Sections and Techniques of the Speech (15)

Sections of a Speech	Techniques Used in a Speech	Techniques the Speaker Uses in the Speech
Introduction	1. Relate the topic to the audience 2. State the importance of your topic 3. Startle the audience 4. Arouse the curiosity of the audience 5. Question the audience 6. Begin with a quotation 7. Tell a story	
Main body	1. Evidence and examples 2. Explanation and analysis 3. Visual aids 4. Personal stories or anecdotes 5. Expert opinions or quotes 6. Transitions	
Conclusion	1. Signal the end of the speech 2. Summarize the speech 3. End with a quotation 4. Make a dramatic statement 5. Refer to the introduction	

Section VI EANLIC Party Tasks

1. Group Work

In groups, research an inspirational role model honored in annual Touching China Awards and deliver a speech about their life and achievements.

2. Prepared Speech

Three students will deliver prepared speeches each week. Score their work according to the feedback checklist below (Table 15.3).

Table 15.3 Checklist (15)

Checklist	Speech 1 1–5 From the least to the most	Speech 2 1–5 From the least to the most	Speech 3 1–5 From the least to the most
Is the speech well-prepared?	1 2 3 4 5	1 2 3 4 5	1 2 3 4 5
Was the speaker's voice loud enough?	1 2 3 4 5	1 2 3 4 5	1 2 3 4 5
Did the speaker look at the audience?	1 2 3 4 5	1 2 3 4 5	1 2 3 4 5
Did the speaker look confident?	1 2 3 4 5	1 2 3 4 5	1 2 3 4 5

continued

Checklist	Speech 1	Speech 2	Speech 3
	1–5 From the least to the most	1–5 From the least to the most	1–5 From the least to the most
Was there a clear and logical structure in the speech?	1 2 3 4 5	1 2 3 4 5	1 2 3 4 5
Were all the major claims supported by evidence?	1 2 3 4 5	1 2 3 4 5	1 2 3 4 5
Have you found any mistakes in grammar/pronunciation?			
Do you have any suggestions for the speaker to improve next time?			

3. Debate

Directions: *Students will work in groups to prepare a claim or counterclaim for the following idea beforehand, and then participate in the debate at the EANLIC Party.*

Some people believe that AI could save education, while others believe that AI could undermine education.

4. Activities Focusing on Words and Expressions

Design an activity using words and expressions from the speech.

Section VII Assignment

Tell a story about "China's Science and Technology".

- Use visual aids in your speech.
- Ensure that your story is well-expressed and engaging.

Unit 16 Learning a Language? Speak It Like You're Playing a Video Game

By Marianna Pascal

Learning Objectives

1. Achieve a thorough understanding of the speech contextually and linguistically.
2. Improve the ability to communicate with others about speaking English.
3. Learn to deliver a speech effectively.
4. Build up confidence to speak English with limited vocabulary.

Text

For the past 20 years, I've been helping Malaysian and other Southeast Asians to speak better English. And through training thousands of Southeast Asians, I've discovered a very surprising truth. *I've discovered that how well somebody communicates in English actually has very little to do with their English level. It has a lot to do with their attitude towards English.* There are people out there who have a very low level of English, and they can communicate very well.

One of them that I remember was a student, a participant of mine, named *Faizal*. He was a factory supervisor—English level very very low—but this guy could just sit and listen to anybody, very calmly, clearly, and then he could respond, and absolutely express his thoughts beautifully, at a very low level of English. So, today I want to share with you what is so different about people like Faizal? How do they do it? And second of all, why is this so important not only to you, but to your children, to your community, and to the future of Malaysia?

And third of all, what's one thing you can do, starting today, if you want to speak with that calm, clear confidence that people like Faizal have. *First of all, what is so different? How do people like Faizal do it?* To answer that question, I'm going to take you back about 10 years, okay? I was training staff at that time, and *my daughter*, at that time, was taking piano lessons. And I started to notice two really strong similarities between my daughter's attitude or thinking towards playing the piano and a lot of Malaysians' thinking or attitude towards English. First of all, I should tell you my daughter absolutely hated piano, hated the lessons, hated practicing. This is my daughter practicing piano, okay? This is as good as it got. This is the real thing. And she dreaded going to piano lessons because to my daughter, going to piano lessons, she was filled with this sort of dread. Because it was all about not screwing up, right? Because like a lot of piano students, to both my daughter and her teacher, her success in piano was measured by how few mistakes she made. At the same time, I noticed that a lot of Malaysians went into English conversations with the same sort of feeling of *dread*. This sort of feeling that they were going to be judged by how many mistakes they were going to make, and whether or not they were going to screw up. Now, the second similarity that I noticed was to do with self-image. My daughter, she knew what good piano sounded like, right? Because we've all heard good piano. And she knew what her level was, and she knew how long she'd have to play for to play like that. And a lot of Malaysians, I noticed, had this idea of what good proper English is supposed to sound like, I see a lot of you nod—and what their English sounded like, and how far they would have to go to get there. And they also felt like they were—like my daughter—just bad, bad piano player, bad English speaker, right? My English not so good, lah. Cannot. Sorry, yah. Cannot. Ah—So I could see these similarities, but I still couldn't figure out, okay, what is it about these people like Faizal, that are so different, that can just do it smoothly, calmly, with confidence? One day, I discovered that answer, and I discovered it quite by chance. It was a day when my computer broke down, and I had to go to a cyber cafe. Okay, it was my first time, and I discovered cyber cafes are disgusting places, okay? They're really gross. They're smelly, and they're filled with boys. And they're all playing noisy, violent games. They're just disgusting places. But I had to go there. So I sat down, and I started noticing this guy beside me. And I became very interested in this guy next to me. Now, this guy is playing this game that is basically, it's like shooting people until they die. And that's it. That's the game, right? And I'm noticing that this guy is not very good. In fact, he's terrible, right? Because I'm looking, and I'm seeing, like, a lot of shooting and … not much dying, right? What really interested me was behind this lousy player were three of his friends, sort of standing there watching him play. What I really noticed was even though this guy was terrible, even though his friends were watching him, there was no embarrassment. There was no feeling of being judged. There was no shyness. In fact, quite the opposite. This guy's totally focused on the bad guys, smile on his face. All he can think about is killing these guys, right? And I'm watching him. And I suddenly realize: this is it. This is the same attitude that people like Faizal have when they speak English, just like this guy. When Faizal goes into an English conversation, he doesn't feel judged. He is entirely focused on the person that he's speaking to and the result he wants to get. He's got no self-awareness, no thoughts about his own mistakes. I want to share with you a real, true example, to paint a picture, of somebody who speaks English like they are playing piano and someone who speaks English like they are playing a computer game. And this is a true story. It happened to me. A while ago, I was in a pharmacy. I had to buy omega; my doctor said I should get omega. And I go to the shelf. There's tons of omega. There's omega that's high in DHA, omega that's high in EPA, and I don't know which one to buy. Now, the sales rep happened to be there. And I saw she's like this well-dressed, professional woman. I walk over to her, and I see this look as she sees me, this sort of— it's a look I recognize very well. Her eyes go all wide. It's sort of that panic: Oh my God! I've got to speak to a native speaker; she's going to judge me and notice my mistakes. I go up to her, and I explain my situation: which omega do I get? And she starts explaining to me everything about DHA and EPA you could possibly imagine. She speaks very quickly, goes all around in circles. And when she finishes, no idea what to buy. So I turn to the girl behind the counter. Now, the girl behind the counter, I heard her before, her English level is very low. But when I walk over to her, this girl, there's no fear. In fact, she's just looking at me. You know that look like ... Yeah? Okay ... So, how? Yeah, I've been in Malaysia for a long time. So, I go up to her and I explain the problem, EPA and DHA.

She looks at me, and she says, "Okay, yeah."

"Ah, EPA for heart."

"DHA for brain."

"Your heart okay or not?"

So I said, "Yeah, yeah." I said, "My heart is really. I think it's pretty good."

She says, "Your brain okay or not?"

I said, "No. No, my brain is not as good as it used to be."

She looks and says, "Okay lah, you take Omega DHA!"

Problem solved, right?

So we've got two different kinds of communicators. We've got the one who's got a high level, but totally focused on herself and getting it right, and therefore, very ineffective. We've got another one, low-level, totally focused on the person she's talking to and getting a result. Effective. And therein lies the difference. Now, why is this distinction so important not just to you, to your children, but to the future of Malaysia and countries like Malaysia? And to answer that, let's take a look at *who actually is speaking English in the world today*, okay? So, if we looked at all of the English conversations in the whole world, taking place right now on planet Earth, we would see that for every native speaker, like me, there are five non-native speakers. And if we'd listen to every conversation in English on planet Earth right now, we would notice that 96% of those conversations involved non-native English speakers—only 4% of those conversations are native speaker to native speaker. This is not my language anymore; this language belongs to you. It's not an art to be mastered; it's just a tool to use to get a result. And I want to give you a real-life example of what English is today in the world, real English today.

This is another true story. I was at a barbecue a little while ago—this was a barbecue for engineers, engineers from all over the world. And they were making hot dogs. Some of the hot dogs were regular hot dogs, and some were these cheese hot dogs, you know, with the cheese in the middle.

A French engineer is cooking the hot dogs, and he turns to this Korean engineer, and he says, "Would you like a hot dog?" And the Korean guy says, "Yes, please!" He says, "Do you want the cheese?" And the Korean guy looks around at the table, he says, "I no see cheese." The French guy says, "The hot dog contains the cheese." The Korean guy doesn't understand him, right? So the French engineer tries again. "The hot dog is ... making from ... with the cheese." The Korean guy still doesn't understand.

He tries again. He says, "The hot dog is coming from—no, the cheese is coming from the hot dog." The Korean guy cannot understand. Now there's a Japanese engineer who's been listening to this conversation, turns to the Korean engineer and he says, "Ah! Cheese ... integrator!" He understands, okay. Everybody understands. So, this is what English is today. It's just a tool to play around with to get a result, like a computer game. Now, the challenge is that we know in schools all around the world, English is not really being taught like it's a tool to play with. It's still being taught like it's an art to master.

And students are judged more on correctness than on clarity. Some of you might remember the old comprehension exam in school. Does everybody remember in school when you'd get a question about a text that you read? You'd have to read through some text, right? And then answer a question to show that you understood the text? And this may have happened to you that you showed you understood the text, but you got a big × because you made a little grammar mistake. Like this student. This student clearly understood paragraph four. But no, not correct! Because he left the letter N off the word "environment". But in the real world, what would matter? In the real world, what would matter is—did you understand the email, or did you understand your customer so that you can go ahead and take action? Now, the problem that I see here, over and over, is that people take the attitude they developed about English in school, and they bring it into their adult life and into their work. And if you're in a stressful situation, and you're having a conversation, and you're trying to give a result to someone and say it correctly, your brain multi-tasks, it cannot do two things at once. And what I see is the brain just shutting down. And you may recognize these three symptoms of the brain shutting down. The first one is that your listening goes. Someone is talking to you, and you're so busy thinking about how you're going to respond and express yourself correctly, you don't actually hear what the other person said. And I can see a lot of nodding in the audience. The second thing to go is your speaking. Your mind sort of shuts down, and that vocabulary you do know just disappears, and the words don't come out. The third thing to go is your confidence. The worst thing about this is you may only be [un]confident because you cannot express yourself clearly, but to the person talking to you, they may misunderstand this as a lack of confidence in your ability to do the job, to perform.

So if you want to speak English like Faizal with that great confidence, here's the one thing that you can do. *When you speak, don't focus on yourself. Focus on the other persons and the result you want to achieve.* Imagine a next generation of Malaysians all with that wonderful confidence in communication that Faizal has at any level of English. Because let's remember that *English today is not an art to be mastered, it's just a tool to use to get a result.* And that tool belongs to you.

Thank you.

Section I Pre-class Tasks

Directions: *Finish the following tasks before class.*

1. Watch and listen to the speech for the first time, and get the main idea of the speech.

2. Watch the speech for the second time and find the answers to the following questions.

（1）How to make your communication sound without enough words preparation?

（2）What truth has the speaker discovered through many years of English language training for Southeast Asians?

（3）How many examples are used in the speech? And what are they?

（4）How has English been taught in schools around the world according to the speaker?

（5）What are your methods of solving the problem of limited vocabulary in your daily life?

3. Design 5 open-ended questions to interview five other students at the English chat. Write down your questions and peer evaluation in Table 16.1.

Table 16.1 Questions and Peer Evaluation (16)

Questions	Peer Evaluation (appropriateness, grammatical accuracy)
1.	
2.	
3.	
4.	
5.	
Student evaluator signature	

Section II Language Focus

1. Words & Expressions

- **supervisor** /ˈsuːpəvaɪzə(r)/ *n.* a supervisor is a person who supervises activities or people, especially workers or students 监督人；指导者；主管人
- **dread** /dred/ *v.* to be very afraid of sth.; to fear that sth. bad is going to happen 非常害怕；极为担心
- **screw up** 弄糟；搞乱；毁坏

- **self-image** /ˌself ˈɪmɪdʒ/ *n.* the opinion or idea you have of yourself, especially of your appearance or abilities 自我形象；自我印象
- **disgusting** /dɪsˈɡʌstɪŋ/ *adj.* extremely unpleasant; unacceptable and shocking 极糟的；令人不快的；令人厌恶的
- **lousy** /ˈlaʊzi/ *adj.* used to show that you feel annoyed or insulted because you do not think that sth. is worth very much（认为某物无太大价值而不满或感到受辱）讨厌的，倒霉的
- **pharmacy** /ˈfɑːməsi/ *n.* a shop or store, or part of one, which sells medicines and drugs 药房；药店；医药柜台
- **ineffective** /ˌɪnɪˈfektɪv/ *adj.* not achieving what you want to achieve; not having any effect 不起作用的；无效果的；无效率的
- **integrator** /ˈɪntɪɡreɪtə/ *n.* a measuring instrument for measuring the area of an irregular plane figure 积分器
- **symptom** /ˈsɪmptəm/ *n.* a change in your body or mind that shows that you are not healthy; a sign that sth. exists, especially sth. bad 症状；征候；征兆

2. Sentences for Further Understanding

Directions: *Translate the following sentences from English into Chinese.*

- I've discovered that how well somebody communicates in English actually has very little to do with their English level. It has a lot to do with their attitude towards English.
- There are people out there who have a very low level of English, and they can communicate very well.
- This guy could just sit and listen to anybody, very calmly, clearly, and then he could respond, absolutely express his thoughts beautifully, at a very low level of English.
- Because like a lot of piano students, to both my daughter and her teacher, her success in piano was measured by how few mistakes she made.
- I started to notice two really strong similarities between my daughter's attitude or thinking towards playing the piano and a lot of Malaysians' thinking or attitude towards English.
- What I really noticed was even though this guy was terrible, even though his friends were watching him, there was no embarrassment.
- When Faizal goes into an English conversation, he doesn't feel judged.
- He is entirely focused on the person that he's speaking to and the result he wants to get.

- When you speak, don't focus on yourself. Focus on the other person and the result you want to achieve.
- Let's remember that English today is not an art to be mastered, it's just a tool to be used to get a result.

Section III Outline of the Speech

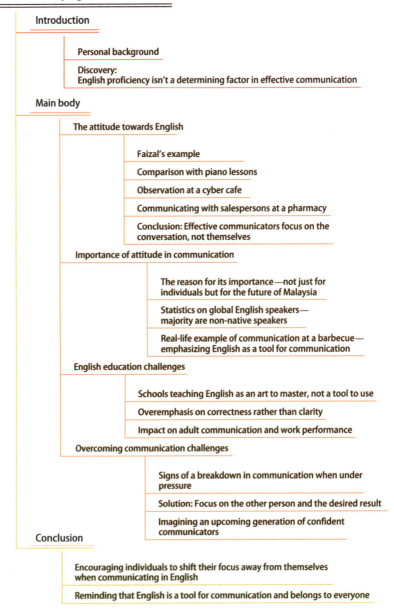

Section IV Public Speaking Skills

Delivering a speech effectively is a valuable skill that can help you convey your message, engage your audience, and leave a lasting impact. Here are some tips on how to deliver a speech with confidence and effectiveness.

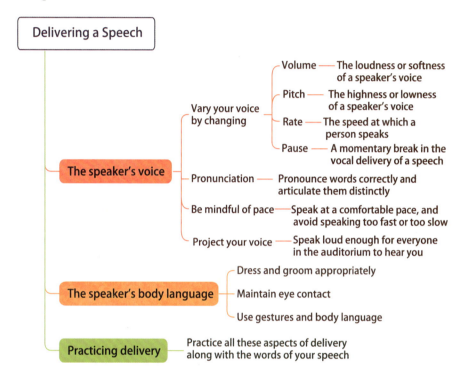

Section V English Chat Tasks

1. Q&A (5 questions): Work in groups to ask and answer questions prepared in the pre-class task.

2. A complete speech includes an introduction, main body and conclusion (Table 16.2). There are many techniques a speaker can use to create these parts of a speech. Discuss in groups what specific techniques the speaker uses in this speech and write down your answers.

Table 16.2 Sections and Techniques of the Speech (16)

Sections of a Speech	Techniques Used in a Speech	Techniques the Speaker Uses in the Speech
Introduction	1. Relate the topic to the audience 2. State the importance of your topic 3. Startle the audience 4. Arouse the curiosity of the audience 5. Question the audience 6. Begin with a quotation 7. Tell a story	
Main body	1. Evidence and examples 2. Explanation and analysis 3. Visual aids 4. Personal stories or anecdotes 5. Expert opinions or quotes 6. Transitions	
Conclusion	1. Signal the end of the speech 2. Summarize the speech 3. End with a quotation 4. Make a dramatic statement 5. Refer to the introduction	

Section VI EANLIC Party Tasks

1. Group Work

In groups, research an inspirational role model honored in annual Touching China Awards and deliver a speech about their life and achievements.

2. Prepared Speech

Three students will deliver prepared speeches each week. Score their work according to the feedback checklist below (Table 16.3).

Table 16.3 Checklist (16)

Checklist	Speech 1 1–5 From the least to the most	Speech 2 1–5 From the least to the most	Speech 3 1–5 From the least to the most
Is the speech well-prepared?	1 2 3 4 5	1 2 3 4 5	1 2 3 4 5
Was the speaker's voice loud enough?	1 2 3 4 5	1 2 3 4 5	1 2 3 4 5
Did the speaker look at the audience?	1 2 3 4 5	1 2 3 4 5	1 2 3 4 5
Did the speaker look confident?	1 2 3 4 5	1 2 3 4 5	1 2 3 4 5

Learning a Language? Speak It Like You're Playing a Video Game

continued

Checklist	Speech 1	Speech 2	Speech 3
	1–5 From the least to the most	1–5 From the least to the most	1–5 From the least to the most
Was there a clear and logical structure in the speech?	1 2 3 4 5	1 2 3 4 5	1 2 3 4 5
Were all the major claims supported by evidence?	1 2 3 4 5	1 2 3 4 5	1 2 3 4 5
Have you found any mistakes in grammar/pronunciation?			
Do you have any suggestions for the speaker to improve next time?			

3. Debate

Directions: *Work in groups to prepare a claim or counterclaim for the following idea beforehand, and then participate in the debate at the EANLIC Party.*

Some people believe that English should be taught as an art to master in school, while others think that English should be taught as a tool to play with.

4. Activities Focusing on Words and Expressions

Design an activity using words and expressions from the speech.

Section VII Assignment

Prepare a speech on "How to Speak English with Limited Vocabulary?". Address the following questions:

- How do you feel when you are unable to communicate in English?
- What are your methods of solving the problem of limited English vocabulary in your daily life?

Unit 17 I Am Not Your Asian Stereotype

By Canwen Xu

Learning Objectives

1. Achieve a thorough understanding of the speech contextually and linguistically.
2. Learn to express yourselves more freely on the topic of identity.
3. Be able to write a persuasive speech.
4. Enhance college students' self-identity and confidence.

Text

My name is Canwen, and I play both the piano and the violin. I aspire to some day be a doctor, and my favorite subject is calculus. My mom and dad are tiger parents, who won't let me go to sleepovers, but they make up for it by serving my favorite meal every single day. Rice. *And I'm a really bad driver.* So my question for you now is, "How long did it take you to figure out I was joking?" As you've probably guessed, today I am going to talk about *race* and I'll start off by sharing with you my story of growing up *Asian-American.* I moved to the United States when I was two years old, so almost *my entire life has been a blend of two cultures.* I eat pasta with chopsticks. I'm addicted to orange chicken, and my childhood hero was Yao Ming. But having grown up in *North Dakota, South Dakota, and Idaho, all states with incredible little racial diversity, it was difficult to reconcile my so-called exotic Chinese heritage with my mainstream American self.* Used to being the only Asian in the room, I was self-conscious at the first thing people noticed about me was, that I wasn't white. And as a child I quickly began to realize that I had two options in front of me. *Conformed to the stereotype that was expected of me, or conformed to the whiteness that surrounded me. There was no in between.* For me, this meant that I always felt self-conscious about being good at math, because people would just say it was because I was Asian, not because I actually worked hard. It meant that whenever a boy asked me out, it was because he had the yellow fever, and not because he actually liked me. *It meant that for the longest time my identity had formed around the fact that I was different.* And I thought that being Asian was the only special thing about me. These effects were emphasized by the places where I lived. Don't get me wrong. Only a small percentage of people were actually *racist*, or, even *borderline racist*, but the vast majority were just a little bit *clueless*. Now, I know you are probably thinking, "What's the difference?" Well, here is an example. Not racist can sound like, "I'm white and you're not." Racist can sound like, "I'm white, you're not, and that makes me better than you." But clueless sounds like, "I'm white, you're not, and I don't know how to deal with that." Now, I don't doubt for a second that these *clueless people* are still nice individuals with great intentions. But they do ask some questions that become pretty annoying after a while. Here are a few examples. "You're Chinese. Oh my goodness, I have a Chinese friend. Do you know him?" "No, I don't know him. Because contrary to your unrealistic expectations, I do not know every single one of the 1.35 billion Chinese people who live on Planet Earth." People also tend to ask, "Where does your name come from?", and I really don't know how to answer that, so I usually stick with the truth. "My parents gave it to me. Where does your name come from?" Don't even get me started on how many times people have confused me with a different Asian person. One time someone came up to me and said, "Angie, I love your art work!" And I was super confused, so I just thanked him and walked away. But, out of all the questions my favorite one is still the classic, "Where are you from?", because I've lived in quite a few places, so this is how the conversation usually goes. "Where are you from?" "Oh, I am from Boise, Idaho." "I see, but where are you really from?" "I mean, I lived in South Dakota for a while." "Okay, what about before that?" "I mean, I lived in North Dakota." "Okay, I'm just going to cut straight to the chase here, I guess what I'm saying is—have you ever lived anywhere far away from here, where people talk a little differently?" "Oh, I know where you talking about, yes, I have, I used to live in Texas." By then, they usually have just given up and wonder to themselves why I'm not one of the cool Asians like Jeremy Lin or Jackie Chan, or they skip the needless banter and go straight for the, "Where is your family from?" So, just an FYI for all of you out there, that is the safest strategy. But, *as amusing as these interactions were, oftentimes they made me want to reject my own culture, because I thought it helped me conform.* I distanced myself from the Asian stereotype as much as possible, by degrading my own race, and pretending I hated math. And the worse part was, it worked. The more I rejected my Chinese identity, the more popular I became. My peers liked me more, because I was more similar to them. I became more confident, because I knew I was more similar to them. But *as I became more Americanized, I also began to lose bits and pieces of myself, parts of me that I can never get back, and no matter how much I tried to pretend that I was the same as my American classmates, I wasn't.* Because for people who have lived in the places where I lived, *white is the norm, and for me, white became the norm too.* For my fourteenth birthday, I received the video game The Sims 3, which lets you create your own characters and control their lives. My fourteen-year-old self created the perfect little mainstream family, complete with a huge mansion and an enormous swimming pool. I binge-played the game for about three months, then put it away and never really thought about it again, until a few weeks ago, when I came to a sudden realization. The family, that I had custom-designed, was white. The character that I had designed for myself, was white. Everyone I had designed was white. And the worst part was, this was by no means a conscious decision that I had made. Never once did I think to myself that I could actually make the characters look like me. Without even thinking, white had become my norm too. *The truth is, Asian Americans play a strange role in the American melting pot. We are the model minority.* Society uses our success to pit us against other people of color as justification that *racism* doesn't exist. But what does that mean to us, *Asian Americans? It means that we are not quite similar enough to be accepted, but we aren't different enough to be loathed. We are in a perpetually grey zone, and society isn't quite sure what to do with us.* So they group us by the color of our skin. They tell us that we must reject our own heritages, so we can fit in with the crowd. They tell us that our foreignness is the only identifying characteristic of us. They strip away our identities one by one, until we are foreign, but not quite foreign, American but not quite American, individual, but only when there are no other people from our native country around. I wish that I had always had the courage to speak out about these issues. But coming from one culture that avoids confrontation, and another that is divided over race, how do I overcome the pressure to keep the peace, while also staying true to who I am? And as much as I hate to admit it, often times I don't speak out, because, if I do, it's at the risk of being told that I am too sensitive, or that I get offended too easily, or that it's just not worth it. But I would point, are people willing to admit that? Yes, *race issues are controversial.* But that's precisely the reason why we need to talk about them. I just turned eighteen, and there are still so many things that I don't know about the world.

But what I do know is that it's hard to admit that you might be part of the problem, that, all of us might be part of the problem. So, *instead of giving you a step-by-step guide on how to not be racist towards Asians, I will let you decide what to take from this talk. All I can do, is share my story.* My name is Canwen, my favorite color is purple. And I play the piano, but not so much the violin. I have two incredibly supportive, hard-working parents, and one very awesome ten-year-old brother. I love calculus more than anything, despise eating rice, and I'm a horrendous driver. *But most of all, I am proud of who I am. A little bit American, a little bit Chinese, and a whole lot of both.*

Thank you.

Section I Pre-class Tasks

Directions: *Finish the following tasks before class.*

1. Watch and listen to the speech for the first time, and get the main idea of the speech.

2. Watch the speech for the second time and find the answers to the following questions.

(1) What is the stereotype of Asian-American in an American eyes?

(2) What do "racist" and "clueless" mean in the speech?

(3) How much do you know about the speaker after listening to her speech?

(4) How should we deal with the stereotype?

(5) What type of speech does this speech belong to?

3. Design 5 open-ended questions to interview five other students at the English chat. Write down your questions and peer evaluation in Table 17.1.

Table 17.1 Questions and Peer Evaluation (17)

Questions	Peer Evaluation (appropriateness, grammatical accuracy)
1.	
2.	
3.	
4.	
5.	
Student evaluator signature	

Section II Language Focus

1. Words & Expressions

- **aspire** /əˈspaɪə(r)/ *v.* to have a strong desire to achieve or to become sth. 渴望（成就）；有志（成为）

- **calculus** /ˈkælkjələs/ *n.* the branch of mathematics that is concerned with limits and with the differentiation and integration of functions 微积分

- **sleepover** /ˈsliːpəʊvə(r)/ *n.* a party for children or young people when a group of them spend the night at one house （儿童或年轻人在某人家玩乐并过夜的）聚会

- **incredible** /ɪnˈkredəbl/ *adj.* impossible or very difficult to believe 不能相信的；难以置信的

- **diversity** /daɪˈvɜːsəti/ *n.* the quality or fact of including a range of many people or things 多样性；多样化

- **reconcile** /ˈrekənsaɪl/ *v.* to find an acceptable way of dealing with two or more ideas, needs, etc. that seem to be opposed to each other 使和谐一致；调和；使配合

- **exotic** /ɪɡˈzɒtɪk/ *adj.* from or in another country, especially a tropical one; seeming exciting and unusual because it is connected with foreign countries 来自异国（尤指热带国家）的；奇异的；异国情调的；异国风味的

- **mainstream** /ˈmeɪnstriːm/ *n.* the ideas and opinions that are thought to be normal because they are shared by most people; the people whose ideas and opinions are most accepted 主流思想；主流群体

- **conform** /kənˈfɔːm/ *v.* to behave and think in the same way as most other people in a group or society 顺从，顺应（大多数人或社会）；随潮流

- **racist** /ˈreɪsɪst/ *n.* a person with a prejudiced belief that one race is superior to others 种族主义者

- **clueless** /ˈkluːləs/ *adj.* very stupid; not able to understand or to do sth. 很愚蠢的；（对某事）不懂的，无能的

- **stereotype** /ˈsteriətaɪp/ *n.* a fixed idea or image that many people have of a particular type of person or thing, but which is often not true in reality 模式化观念（或形象）；老一套；刻板印象

- **degrading** /dɪˈɡreɪdɪŋ/ *adj.* treating sb. as if they have no value, so that they lose their self-respect and the respect of other people 有辱人格的；贬低的

- **Americanize** /əˈmerɪkənaɪz/ *v.* to make sb./sth. American in character 使美国化

- **conscious** /ˈkɒnʃəs/ *adj.* aware of sth.; noticing sth. 意识到；注意到
- **norm** /nɔːm/ *n.* a situation or a pattern of behaviour that is usual or expected 常态；正常行为
- **justification** /ˌdʒʌstɪfɪˈkeɪʃn/ *n.* a good reason why sth. exists or is done 正当理由
- **loathe** /ləʊð/ *v.* to dislike sb./sth. very much 极不喜欢；厌恶
- **perpetually** /pəˈpetʃuəli/ *adv.* everlastingly 永久地
- **strip** /strɪp/ *v.* to remove a layer from sth., especially so that it is completely exposed 除去，剥去（一层）；（尤指）剥光
- **confrontation** /ˌkɒnfrʌnˈteɪʃn/ *n.* a situation in which there is an angry disagreement between people or groups who have different opinions 对抗；对峙；冲突
- **controversial** /ˌkɒntrəˈvɜːʃl/ *adj.* causing a lot of angry public discussion and disagreement 引起争论的；有争议的
- **horrendous** /həˈrendəs/ *adj.* extremely shocking 令人震惊的；骇人的

2. Sentences for Further Understanding

Directions：*Translate the following sentences from English into Chinese.*

- But having grown up in North Dakota, South Dakota, and Idaho, all states with incredible little racial diversity, it was difficult to reconcile my so-called exotic Chinese heritage with my mainstream American self.
- But, as amusing as these interactions were, oftentimes they made me want to reject my own culture, because I thought it helped me conform.
- I distanced myself from the Asian stereotype as much as possible, by degrading my own race, and pretending I hated math.
- It meant that for the longest time my identity had formed around the fact that I was different.
- The more I rejected my Chinese identity, the more popular I became.
- But as I became more Americanized, I also began to lose bits and pieces of myself, parts of me that I can never get back, and no matter how much I tried to pretend that I was the same as my American classmates, I wasn't.
- Society uses our success to pit us against other people of color as justification that racism doesn't exist.
- They strip away our identities one by one, until we are foreign, but not quite foreign, American but not quite American, individual, but only when there are no other people from our native country around.

- But coming from one culture that avoids confrontation, and another that is divided over race, how do I overcome the pressure to keep the peace, while also staying true to who I am?
- And as a child I quickly began to realize that I had two options in front of me. Conformed to the stereotype that was expected of me, or conformed to the whiteness that surrounded me.

Section III Outline of the Speech

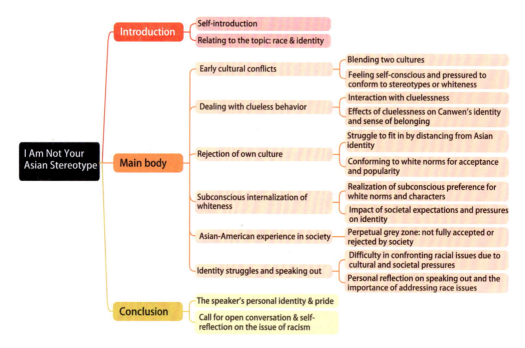

Section IV Public Speaking Skills

A persuasive speech is a type of speech that aims to convince the audience of a particular point of view or persuade them to take a specific action or adopt a particular belief. It typically involves presenting arguments, evidence, and reasoning to influence the audience's thoughts or behavior. Persuasive speeches are often delivered in various settings, including political campaigns, sales pitches, debates, and public speaking events.

Unit 17
I Am Not Your Asian Stereotype

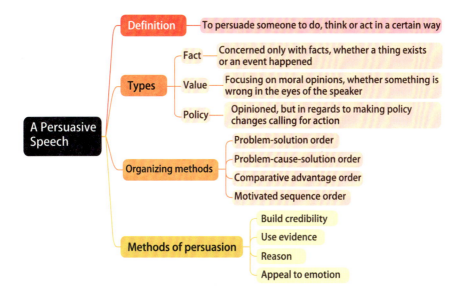

Section V English Chat Tasks

1. Q&A (5 questions): Work in groups to ask and answer questions prepared in the pre-class task.

2. A complete speech includes an introduction, main body and conclusion (Table 17.2). There are many techniques a speaker can use to create these parts of a speech. Discuss in groups what specific techniques the speaker uses in this speech and write down your answers.

Table 17.2 Sections and Techniques of the Speech (17)

Sections of a Speech	Techniques Used in a Speech	Techniques the Speaker Uses in the Speech
Introduction	1. Relate the topic to the audience 2. State the importance of your topic 3. Startle the audience 4. Arouse the curiosity of the audience 5. Question the audience 6. Begin with a quotation 7. Tell a story	
Main body	1. Evidence and examples 2. Explanation and analysis 3. Visual aids 4. Personal stories or anecdotes 5. Expert opinions or quotes 6. Transitions	

continued

Sections of a Speech	Techniques Used in a Speech	Techniques the Speaker Uses in the Speech
Conclusion	1. Signal the end of the speech 2. Summarize the speech 3. End with a quotation 4. Make a dramatic statement 5. Refer to the introduction	

Section VI EANLIC Party Tasks

1. Group Work

In groups, research an inspirational role model honored in annual Touching China Awards and deliver a speech about their life and achievements.

2. Prepared Speech

Three students will deliver prepared speeches each week. Score their work according to the feedback checklist below (Table 17.3).

Table 17.3 Checklist (17)

Checklist	Speech 1 1–5 From the least to the most	Speech 2 1–5 From the least to the most	Speech 3 1–5 From the least to the most
Is the speech well-prepared?	1 2 3 4 5	1 2 3 4 5	1 2 3 4 5
Was the speaker's voice loud enough?	1 2 3 4 5	1 2 3 4 5	1 2 3 4 5
Did the speaker look at the audience?	1 2 3 4 5	1 2 3 4 5	1 2 3 4 5
Did the speaker look confident?	1 2 3 4 5	1 2 3 4 5	1 2 3 4 5
Was there a clear and logical structure in the speech?	1 2 3 4 5	1 2 3 4 5	1 2 3 4 5
Were all the major claims supported by evidence?	1 2 3 4 5	1 2 3 4 5	1 2 3 4 5
Have you found any mistakes in grammar/pronunciation?			
Do you have any suggestions for the speaker to improve next time?			

3. Debate

Directions: *Students will work in groups to prepare a claim or counterclaim for the following idea beforehand, and then participate in the debate at the EANLIC Party.*

In order to survive in a new host culture, some people try to completely change their original cultural identity. Is it a positive or negative response to living in a new culture?

4. Activities Focusing on Words and Expressions

Design an activity using words and expressions from the speech.

Section VII Assignment

Prepare a speech on "What Are the Stereotypes of Chinese and Asians?" Address the following questions and requirements:

- What is a stereotype?
- What are the stereotypes of Chinese and Asians?

Offer personal insights into ways to avoid stereotypes. Ensure that your story is well-expressed and engaging.

Unit 18 How Societies Can Grow Old Better

By Jared Diamond

Learning Objectives

1. Achieve a thorough understanding of the speech contextually and linguistically.
2. Improve the ability to communicate with others about aging.
3. Be able to write an informative speech.
4. Develop an appreciation for contributions the elderly make in society.

Text

To give me an idea of how many of you here may find what I'm about to tell you of practical value, let me ask you please to raise your hands: Who here is either over 65 years old or hopes to live past age 65 or has parents or grandparents who did live or have lived past 65, raise your hands, please.

Okay. You are the people to whom my talk will be of practical value. The rest of you won't find my talk personally relevant, but I think that you will still find the subject fascinating.

I'm going to talk about growing older in traditional societies. This subject constitutes just one chapter of my latest book, which compares traditional, small, tribal societies with our large, modern societies, with respect to many topics such as bringing up children, growing older, health, dealing with danger, settling disputes, religion and speaking more than one language.

Those tribal societies, which constituted all human societies for most of human history, are far more *diverse* than are our modern, recent, big societies. All big societies that have governments, and where most people are strangers to each other, are inevitably similar to each other and different from tribal societies. Tribes constitute thousands of natural experiments in how to run a human society. They constitute experiments from which we ourselves may be able to learn. Tribal societies shouldn't be scorned as primitive and miserable, but also they shouldn't be romanticized as happy and peaceful. When we learn of tribal practices, some of them will horrify us, but there are other tribal practices which, when we hear about them, we may admire and envy and wonder whether we could adopt those practices ourselves.

Most old people in the U.S. end up living separately from their children and from most of their friends of their earlier years, and often they live in separate retirements homes for the elderly, whereas *in traditional societies, older people instead live out their lives among their children, their other relatives, and their lifelong friends.* Nevertheless, *the treatment of the elderly varies enormously among traditional societies, from much worse to much better than in our modern societies.*

At the worst extreme, many traditional societies get rid of their elderly in one of four increasingly direct ways: by neglecting their elderly and not feeding or cleaning them until they die, or by abandoning them when the group moves, or by encouraging older people to commit suicide, or by killing older people. In which tribal societies do children abandon or kill their parents? It happens mainly under two conditions. One is in nomadic, hunter-gather societies that often shift camp and that are physically incapable of transporting old people who can't walk when the able-bodied younger people already have to carry their young children and all their physical possessions. The other condition is in societies living in marginal or fluctuating environments, such as the Arctic or deserts, where there are periodic food shortages, and occasionally there just isn't enough food to keep everyone alive. Whatever food is available has to be reserved for able-bodied adults and for children. To us Americans, it sounds horrible to think of abandoning or killing your own sick wife or husband or elderly mother or father, but what could those traditional societies do differently? They face a cruel situation of no choice. Their old people had to do it to their own parents, and the old people know what now is going to happen to them.

At the opposite extreme in treatment of the elderly, *the happy extreme*, are the New Guinea farming societies where I've been doing my fieldwork for the past 50 years, and most other sedentary traditional societies around the world. In those societies, older people are cared for. They are fed. They remain valuable. And they continue to live in the same hut or else in a nearby hut near their children, relatives and lifelong friends.

There are two main sets of reasons for this variation among societies in their treatment of old people. The variation depends especially on the usefulness of old people and on the society's values.

First, as regards usefulness, older people continue to perform useful services. One use of older people in traditional societies is that they often are still effective at producing food. Another traditional usefulness of older people is that they are capable of babysitting their grandchildren, thereby freeing up their own adult children, the parents of those grandchildren, to go hunting and gathering food for the grandchildren. Still another traditional value of older people is in making tools, weapons, baskets, pots and textiles. In fact, they're usually the people who are best at it. Older people usually are the leaders of traditional societies, and the people most knowledgeable about politics, medicine, religion, songs and dances.

Finally, older people in traditional societies have a huge significance that would never occur to us in our modern, literate societies, where our sources of information are books and the Internet. In contrast, in traditional societies without writing, older people are the repositories of information. It's their knowledge that spells the difference between survival and death for their whole society in a time of crisis caused by rare events for which only the oldest people alive have had experience. Those, then, are the ways in which older people are useful in traditional societies. Their usefulness varies and contributes to variation in the society's treatment of the elderly.

The other set of reasons for variation in the treatment of the elderly is the society's cultural values. For example, there's particular emphasis on respect for the elderly in East Asia, associated with Confucius' doctrine of *filial piety*, which means obedience, respect and support for elderly parents. Cultural values that emphasize respect for older people contrast with the low status of the elderly in the U.S. Older Americans are at a big disadvantage in job applications. They're at a big disadvantage in hospitals. Our hospitals have an explicit policy called age-based allocation of healthcare resources. That sinister expression means that if hospital resources are limited, for example, if only one donor heart becomes available for transplant, or if a surgeon has time to operate on only a certain number of patients, American hospitals have an explicit policy of giving preference to younger patients over older patients on the grounds that younger patients are considered more valuable to society because they have more years of life ahead of them, even though the younger patients have fewer years of valuable life experience behind them. There are several reasons for this low status of the elderly in the U.S. One is our Protestant work ethic which places high value on work, so older people who are no longer working aren't respected. Another reason is our American emphasis on the virtues of self-reliance and independence, so we instinctively look down on older people who are no longer self-reliant and independent. Still a third reason is our American cult of youth, which shows up even in our advertisements. Ads for Coca-Cola and beer always depict smiling young people, even though old as well as young people buy and drink Coca-Cola and beer. Just think, what's the last time you saw a Coke or beer ad depicting smiling people 85 years old? Never. Instead, the only American ads featuring white-haired old people are ads for retirement homes and pension planning.

Well, what has changed in the status of the elderly today compared to their status in traditional societies? *There have been a few changes for the better and more changes for the worse. Big changes for the better* include the fact that today we enjoy much longer lives, much better health in our old age, and much better recreational opportunities. *Another change for the better* is that we now have specialized retirement facilities and programs to take care of old people. *Changes for the worse* begin with the cruel reality that we now have more old people and fewer young people than at any time in the past. That means that all those old people are more of a burden on the few young people, and that each old person has less individual value. *Another big change for the worse* in the status of the elderly is the breaking of social ties with age, because older people, their children, and their friends, all move and scatter independently of each other many times during their lives. We Americans move on the average every five years. Hence our older people are likely to end up living distantly from their children and the friends of their youth. Yet another change for the worse in the status of the elderly is formal retirement from the workforce, carrying with it a loss of work friendships and a loss of the self-esteem associated with work. Perhaps *the biggest change for the worse* is that our elderly are objectively less useful than in traditional societies. Widespread literacy means that they are no longer useful as repositories of knowledge. When we want some information, we look it up in a book or we Google it instead of finding some old person to ask. The slow pace of technological change in traditional societies means that what someone learns there as a child is still useful when that person is old, but the rapid pace of technological change today means that what we learn as children is no longer useful 60 years later. And conversely, we older people are not fluent in the technologies essential for surviving in modern society. For example, as a 15-year-old, I was considered outstandingly good at multiplying numbers because I had memorized the multiplication tables and I know how to use logarithms and I'm quick at manipulating a slide rule. Today, though, those skills are utterly useless because any idiot can now multiply eight-digit numbers accurately and instantly with a pocket calculator. Conversely, I at age 75 am incompetent at skills essential for everyday life. My family's first TV set in 1948 had only three knobs that I quickly mastered: an on-off switch, a volume knob, and a channel selector knob. Today, just to watch a program on the TV set in my own house, I have to operate a 41-button TV remote that utterly defeats me. I have to telephone my 25-year-old sons and ask them to talk me through it while I try to push those wretched 41 buttons.

What can we do to improve the lives of the elderly in the U.S., and to make better use of their value? That's a huge problem. In my remaining four minutes today, *I can offer just a few suggestions. One value of older people is that they are increasingly useful as grandparents for offering high-quality childcare to their grandchildren*, if they choose to do it, as more young women enter the workforce and as fewer young parents of either gender stay home as full-time caretakers of their children. Compared to the usual alternatives of paid babysitters and daycare centers, grandparents offer superior, motivated, experienced child care. They've already gained experience from raising their own children. They usually love their grandchildren, and are eager to spend time with them. Unlike other caregivers, grandparents don't quit their job because they found another job with higher pay looking after another baby. *A second value of older people is paradoxically related to their loss of value as a result of changing world conditions and technology.* At the same time, older people have gained in value today precisely because of their unique experience of living conditions that have now become rare because of rapid change, but that could come back. For example, only Americans now in their 70s or older today can remember the experience of living through a great depression, the experience of living through a world war, and agonizing whether or not dropping atomic bombs would be more horrible than the likely consequences of not dropping atomic bombs. Most of our current voters and politicians have no personal experience of any of those things, but millions of older Americans do. Unfortunately, all of those terrible situations could come back. Even if they don't come back, we have to be able to plan for them on the basis of the experience of what they were like. *Older people have that experience. Younger people don't.*

The remaining value of older people that I'll mention involves recognizing that while there are many things that older people can no longer do, there are other things that they can do better than younger people. A challenge for society is to make use of those things that older people are better at doing. Some abilities, of course, decrease with age. Those include abilities at tasks requiring physical strength and stamina, ambition, and the power of novel reasoning in a circumscribed situation, such as figuring out the structure of DNA, best left to scientists under the age of 30. Conversely, valuable attributes that increase with age include experience, understanding of people and human relationships, ability to help other people without your own ego getting in the way, and interdisciplinary thinking about large databases, such as economics and comparative history, best left to scholars over the age of 60. *Hence older people are much better than younger people at supervising, administering, advising, strategizing, teaching, synthesizing, and devising long-term plans.* I've seen this value of older people with so many of my friends in their 60s, 70s, 80s and 90s, who are still active as investment managers, farmers, lawyers and doctors. *In short, many traditional societies make better use of their elderly and give their elderly more satisfying lives than we do in modern, big societies.*

Paradoxically nowadays, when we have more elderly people than ever before, living healthier lives and with better medical care than ever before, old age is in some respects more miserable than ever before. The lives of the elderly are widely recognized as constituting a disaster area of modern American society. *We can surely do better by learning from the lives of the elderly in traditional societies.* But what's true of the lives of the elderly in traditional societies is true of many other features of traditional societies as well. Of course, I'm not advocating that we all give up agriculture and metal tools and return to a hunter-gatherer lifestyle. There are many obvious respects in which our lives today are far happier than those in small, traditional societies. To mention just a few examples, our lives are longer, materially much richer, and less plagued by violence than are the lives of people in traditional societies. But there are also things to be admired about people in traditional societies, and perhaps to be learned from them. Their lives are usually socially much richer than our lives, although materially poorer. Their children are more self-confident, more independent, and more socially skilled than are our children. They think more realistically about dangers than we do. They almost never die of diabetes, heart disease, stroke, and the other noncommunicable diseases that will be the causes of death of almost all of us in this room today. Features of the modern lifestyle predispose us to those diseases, and features of the traditional lifestyle protect us against them.

Those are just some examples of what we can learn from traditional societies. I hope that you will find it as fascinating to read about traditional societies as I found it to live in those societies.

Thank you.

Section I Pre-class Tasks

Directions: *Finish the following tasks before class.*

1. Watch and listen to the speech for the first time, and get the main idea of the speech.

2. Watch the speech for the second time and find the answers to the following questions.

(1) What kind of ways can be used to make the elderly more valuable?

(2) According to Jared Diamond, how do traditional societies get rid of their elderly? Why do they have to do so?

(3) What factors influence the treatment of the elderly in traditional societies?

(4) From Jared Diamond's perspective, what are the values of the elderly in America today?

(5) What do you think are the problems the elderly face in our society now? What are the possible ways to solve them?

3. Design 5 open-ended questions to interview five other students at the English chat. Write down your questions and peer evaluation in Table 18.1.

Table 18.1 Questions and Peer Evaluation (18)

Questions	Peer Evaluation (appropriateness, grammatical accuracy)
1.	
2.	
3.	
4.	
5.	
Student evaluator signature	

Section II Language Focus

1. Words & Expressions

- **practical** /ˈpræktɪkl/ *adj.* connected with real situations rather than with ideas or theories 实际的；切实可行的

- **relevant** /ˈreləvənt/ *adj.* closely connected with the subject you are discussing or the situation you are thinking about 相关的；切题的

- **constitute** /ˈkɒnstɪtjuːt/ *v.* to be the parts that together form sth.; to be considered to be sth. 组成，构成；被看做是

- **tribal** /ˈtraɪbl/ *adj.* relating to or characteristic of a tribe 部落的；（尤指南亚的）部落成员的
- **dispute** /dɪˈspjuːt/ *n.* an argument or a disagreement between two people, groups or countries; discussion about a subject where there is disagreement 争端；纠纷
- **diverse** /daɪˈvɜːs/ *adj.* very different from each other and of various kinds 多种多样的；形形色色的
- **inevitably** /ɪnˈevɪtəbli/ *adv.* as is certain to happen 不可避免地；必然地
- **primitive** /ˈprɪmətɪv/ *adj.* belonging to an early stage in the development of humans or animals 原始的；人类或动物发展早期的
- **romanticize** /rəʊˈmæntɪsaɪz/ *v.* to make sth. seem more attractive or interesting than it really is 使浪漫化；使传奇化；使更加富有吸引力
- **abandon** /əˈbændən/ *vt.* to leave sb. especially sb. you are responsible for, with no intention of returning（不顾责任、义务等）离弃；遗弃；抛弃
- **babysit** /ˈbeɪbisɪt/ *v.* to take care of babies or children for a short time while their parents are out 代人临时照看小孩；当临时保姆
- **variation** /ˌveəriˈeɪʃn/ *n.* a change, especially in the amount or level of sth.（数量、水平等的）变化；变更；变异
- **doctrine** /ˈdɒktrɪn/ *n.* a belief or set of beliefs held and taught by a Church, a political party, etc. 教义；主义；学说；信条
- **instinctively** /ɪnˈstɪŋktɪvli/ *adv.* an instinctive feeling, idea, or action is one that you have or do without thinking or reasoning 本能地；凭直觉地
- **depict** /dɪˈpɪkt/ *n.* to describe sth. in words, or give an impression of sth in words or with a picture 描写；描述；刻画
- **literacy** /ˈlɪtərəsi/ *n.* the ability to read and write 读写能力
- **repository** /rɪˈpɒzətri/ *n.* a place where sth. is stored in large quantities 仓库；贮藏室；存放处
- **interdisciplinary** /ˌɪntədɪsəˈplɪnəri/ *adj.* involving different areas of knowledge or study 多学科的；跨学科的
- **noncommunicable** /ˌnɒnkəˈmjuːnɪkəbl/ *adj.* (of disease) not capable of being passed on 不会传染的

2. Sentences for Further Understanding

Directions：*Translate the following sentences from English into Chinese.*

- You are the people to whom my talk will be of practical value. The rest of you won't

find my talk personally relevant, but I think that you will still find the subject fascinating.
- This subject constitutes just one chapter of my latest book, which compares traditional, small, tribal societies with our large, modern societies, with respect to many topics such as bringing up children, growing older, health, dealing with danger, settling disputes, religion and speaking more than one language.
- All big societies that have governments, and where most people are strangers to each other, are inevitably similar to each other and different from tribal societies. Tribes constitute thousands of natural experiments in how to run a human society.
- Nevertheless, the treatment of the elderly varies enormously among traditional societies, from much worse to much better than in our modern societies.
- At the worst extreme, many traditional societies get rid of their elderly in one of four increasingly direct ways: by neglecting their elderly and not feeding or cleaning them until they die, or by abandoning them when the group moves, or by encouraging older people to commit suicide, or by killing older people.
- It happens mainly under two conditions. One is in nomadic, hunter-gather societies that often shift camp and that are physically incapable of transporting old people who can't walk when the able-bodied younger people already have to carry their young children and all their physical possessions. The other condition is in societies living in marginal or fluctuating environments, such as the Arctic or deserts, where there are periodic food shortages, and occasionally there just isn't enough food to keep everyone alive.
- In those societies, older people are cared for. They are fed. They remain valuable. And they continue to live in the same hut or else in a nearby hut near their children, relatives and lifelong friends.
- Older people in traditional societies have a huge significance that would never occur to us in our modern, literate societies, where our sources of information are books and the Internet.
- There's particular emphasis on respect for the elderly in East Asia, associated with Confucius' doctrine of filial piety, which means obedience, respect and support for elderly parents.
- One is our protestant work ethic which places high value on work, so older people who are no longer working aren't respected. Another reason is our American emphasis on the virtues of self-reliance and independence, so we instinctively look down on older people who are no longer self-reliant and independent.

- There have been a few changes for the better and more changes for the worse.
- Our elderly are objectively less useful than in traditional societies. Widespread literacy means that they are no longer useful as repositories of knowledge.
- One value of older people is that they are increasingly useful as grandparents for offering high-quality childcare to their grandchildren, if they choose to do it, as more young women enter the workforce and as fewer young parents of either gender stay home as full-time caretakers of their children.
- In short, many traditional societies make better use of their elderly and give their elderly more satisfying lives than we do in modern, big societies.
- Paradoxically nowadays, when we have more elderly people than ever before, living healthier lives and with better medical care than ever before, old age is in some respects more miserable than ever before.
- Features of the modern lifestyle predispose us to those diseases, and features of the traditional lifestyle protect us against them.

Section III Outline of the Speech

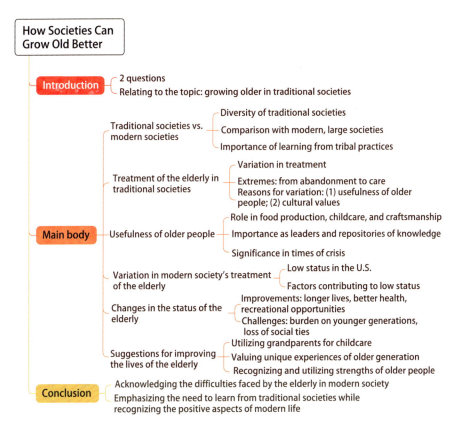

Section IV Public Speaking Skills

An informative speech is a type of presentation that is designed to provide the audience with factual information, knowledge, or insights about a specific topic. The primary goal of an informative speech is to educate, explain, or clarify a subject to the audience in a clear and organized manner. Informative speeches are commonly delivered in educational settings, business presentations, public speaking events, and more.

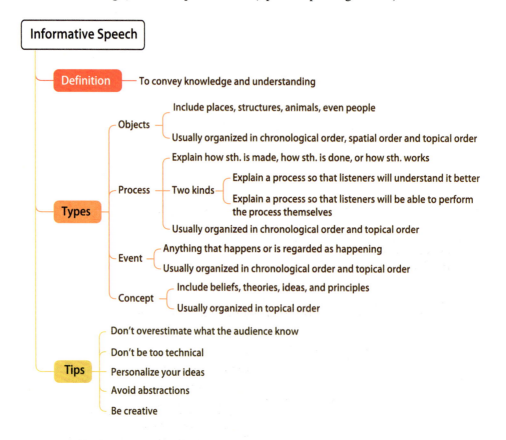

Section V English Chat Tasks

1. Q&A (5 questions): Work in groups to ask and answer questions prepared in the pre-class task.

2. A complete speech includes an introduction, main body and conclusion (Table 18.2). There are many techniques a speaker can use to create these parts of a speech. Discuss in groups what specific techniques the speaker uses in this speech and write down your answers.

Table 18.2　Sections and Techniques of the Speech（18）

Sections of a Speech	Techniques Used in a Speech	Techniques the Speaker Uses in the Speech
Introduction	1. Relate the topic to the audience 2. State the importance of your topic 3. Startle the audience 4. Arouse the curiosity of the audience 5. Question the audience 6. Begin with a quotation 7. Tell a story	
Main body	1. Evidence and examples 2. Explanation and analysis 3. Visual aids 4. Personal stories or anecdotes 5. Expert opinions or quotes 6. Transitions	
Conclusion	1. Signal the end of the speech 2. Summarize the speech 3. End with a quotation 4. Make a dramatic statement 5. Refer to the introduction	

Section VI　EANLIC Party Tasks

1. Group Work

In groups, research an inspirational role model honored in annual Touching China Awards and deliver a speech about their life and achievements.

2. Prepared Speech

Three students will deliver prepared speeches each week. Score their work according to the feedback checklist below (Table 18.3).

Table 18.3　Checklist（18）

Checklist	Speech 1 1–5 From the least to the most	Speech 2 1–5 From the least to the most	Speech 3 1–5 From the least to the most
Is the speech well-prepared?	1　2　3　4　5	1　2　3　4　5	1　2　3　4　5
Was the speaker's voice loud enough?	1　2　3　4　5	1　2　3　4　5	1　2　3　4　5
Did the speaker look at the audience?	1　2　3　4　5	1　2　3　4　5	1　2　3　4　5
Was there a clear and logical structure in the speech?	1　2　3　4　5	1　2　3　4　5	1　2　3　4　5

continued

Checklist	Speech 1	Speech 2	Speech 3
	1–5 From the least to the most	1–5 From the least to the most	1–5 From the least to the most
Did the speaker look confident?	1 2 3 4 5	1 2 3 4 5	1 2 3 4 5
Were all the major claims supported by evidence?	1 2 3 4 5	1 2 3 4 5	1 2 3 4 5
Have you found any mistakes in grammar/pronunciation?			
Do you have any suggestions for the speaker to improve next time?			

3. Debate

Directions: *Work in groups to prepare a claim or counterclaim for the following idea beforehand, and then participate in the debate at the EANLIC Party.*

Should societies prioritize resources for the aging population or focus more on the younger generation?

4. Activities Focusing on Words and Expressions

Design an activity using words and useful expressions from the speech.

Section VII Assignment

Prepare a speech about "How to Deal with the Aging Problem?". Include a personal experience and ensure that your story is well-expressed and engaging.

参考文献

[1] Snow, Ann & Brinton, Donna. *Content-Based Instruction：What Every ESL Teacher Needs to Know*[M]. Michigan：University of Michigan Press ELT, 2023.

[2] Gregory, Hamilton. *Public Speaking for College & Career（12th Edition）*[M]. New York：Mcgraw, 2020.

[3] Bill, Johnston. *Values in English Language Teaching*[M]. London：Routledge, 2002.

[4] Cammarata, Laurent. *Content-Based Foreign Language Teaching：Curriculum and Pedagogy for Developing Advanced Thinking and Literacy Skills*[M]. London：Routledge, 2016.

[5] Lucas, Stephen E. *The Art of Public Speaking（13th Edition）*[M]. Beijing：Foreign Language Teaching and Research Press, 2021.

[6] 段平华, 邓丽萍. 语言探秘ABC[M]. 长春：吉林大学出版社, 2017.

[7] 贺芳, 朱安博. 课程思政视阈下的外语教学研究与实践探索[M]. 北京：首都经济贸易大学出版社, 2023.

[8] 何宁, 王守仁. 口语教程：英语演讲与辩论（一）[M]. 上海：上海外语教育出版社, 2021.

[9] 胡杰辉. 外语课程思政视角下的教学设计研究[J]. 中国外语, 2021（2）：53-59.

[10] Connie Gibson. 英语演讲实训指南[M]. 北京：外语教学与研究出版社, 2008.

[11] 李丹玲. TED演讲视听说1[M]. 北京：清华大学出版社, 2017.

[12] 苗兴伟. 外语课程思政视域下价值引领的实践路径[J]. 外语与外语教学, 2023（6）：20-27, 145-146.

[13] 陶曦. 英语演讲（第二版）[M]. 北京：北京大学出版社, 2023.

[14] 王倩. 英语演讲与辩论[M]. 北京：清华大学出版社, 2022.

[15] 王欣. 英语专业教育改革：课程思政与价值引领[M]. 上海：上海外语教

育出版社，2021.

[16] 徐锦芬，刘文波. 实用英语教学法教程（第二版）[M]. 北京：中国人民大学出版社，2024.

[17] https://www.ted.com/talks.